D0913968

a doctor
among
the
addicts

by NAT HENTOFF

a doctor among the addicts

Rand McNally & Company ⊕

RC 566
.H45

*I have known many real victims
of this artificial tragedy, and this book
is dedicated to them.*

INDIANA
UNIVERSITY
LIBRARY

NORTHWEST

Copyright © 1968 by NAT HENTOFF
Copyright 1967 under International Copyright Union by NAT HENTOFF
All Rights Reserved
Library of Congress Catalog Card Number: 68-11406
Printed in the United States of America by
RAND McNALLY & COMPANY

Third Printing, November, 1970

THE NEW YORK TIMES *of March 11, 1967, told of Angelo Zayas, a 31-year-old unemployed factory worker who lives with his parents, five brothers, and four sisters in Brooklyn. Zayas had broken into a mailbox and then telephoned a postal inspector he knew so that he could be arrested. A narcotics addict, Zayas in his desperation had yielded to the delusion that only in prison could he be treated for his illness. He had already served twenty-seven months in a federal penitentiary for a mail theft he had committed to obtain money for narcotics. In prison he had, of course, been withdrawn from heroin. Upon his release, his craving had returned. Alarmed, he asked parole officers for help. They recommended he enroll in a detoxification program at Manhattan General Hospital. There he was told he would be put on a long waiting list. And so he committed another crime in order to return to prison.*

Said the Assistant United States Attorney handling the case: "It is a tragic situation when an addict has to commit a crime to enable him to secure immediate and proper treatment. There must be many like him walking the streets." It is also tragic that the "treatment" Angelo Zayas will receive in prison is very likely to fail. The odds are that once released, he will become addicted again.

Newsweek—Phil MacMullan

Marie Nyswander

INTRODUCTION

FOR ALL the alarms, and some nascent quasi-religions, which have accompanied the rise in usage of LSD and other hallucinogens, heroin addiction remains a serious and bristlingly controversial problem. The Federal Narcotics Bureau claims there are 59,720 heroin addicts in the United States, but the actual number is at least four or five times more. Some authorities put the figure at one million. Dr. Efrén Ramirez, narcotics coordinator for the City of New York, estimates there are at least 100,000 addicts in that city alone. There were 5,387 arrests in 1966 connected with narcotics use and traffic, an increase of 40 percent over 1965. And, according to New York City Police Commissioner, Howard Leary, "Ten percent of *all* persons arrested in New York City admit being narcotics users." Addicts commit at least 20 percent of all burglaries in New York City—burglaries amounting to more than $1 billion worth of goods and possessions a year.

There is also, of course, an incalculable loss in human beings—the waste of the capacities, potentialities, and spirits of the addicts themselves and the draining anxiety their addiction breeds in their families. Much of that human loss takes place in the slums of our cities, adding to the price Negroes

7

and other minority groups pay for being compressed into ghettos where housing is decayed, education criminally inferior, and jobs meager in terms of both income and pride.

For Dr. Marie Nyswander, whose odyssey among the addicts is the subject of this book, heroin addiction is "an ever-growing problem, particularly among adolescents. I know that according to a Federal Bureau of Narcotics study released in March, 1967, addiction among Negroes has declined in the past decade. But that study makes me wonder again about the accuracy of the Bureau's technique for collecting statistics. And even if there has been a decline among Negroes, so much heroin addiction does remain, and so many lives are still being lost."

For more than a decade, Dr. Nyswander has been the most resourceful, and the most widely experienced, of those few physicians and psychiatrists who have been engaged in trying to find ways to end the despair that has been endemic to heroin addiction. Because of her conception of the addict, she has been regarded as "a romantic" by some of her colleagues. Others dispute her methods. But no doctor in the field has explored so many different routes by which addicts can become functioning members of society. And the results of her most current research into the use of methadone as a catalyst for the rebirth of addicts indicate she and her colleagues have made a major breakthrough in the treatment of many addicted to heroin.

Methadone, a long-acting, synthetic narcotic, blocks the euphoric action of heroin and other opiates. An addict who remains on methadone cannot be readdicted to heroin or any other narcotic. After three years of research, Dr. Vincent P. Dole, who has been associated with Dr. Nyswander in the methadone project in New York since its beginning, disclosed in May, 1967, that of 383 heroin addicts taken into the program, only 33 were dropped from it or left on their own. The rest, many of them for the first time in their lives, have become self-supporting, responsible members of the community.

Methadone is not *the* answer to heroin addiction. Other alternative approaches may be more effective for some addicts; but methadone, as I shall indicate, can make a radically qualitative difference in the lives of many addicts and it can also make possible new dimensions of research into the nature of addiction.

This book is not only an exploration of Dr. Nyswander's discoveries and myth-destroying expeditions among the addicts. It is also about Dr. Nyswander herself—a singularly resilient and open woman whose work with addicts has led her to a number of fundamental questions about the values of the "normal" members of this society. Rather than being a "romantic," she is unusually cognizant of the ambiguities and the evasions chronic to the way most of us now live. And she is aware of the various addictions to which many of us are bound — addictions to myth, to "happiness" as the act of consumption, to life as resignation.

While there are references to the methadone treatment throughout the book, a full-scale chapter on the origin and current status of that project does not appear until close to the end. I did this because the importance of the methadone breakthrough can be seen most clearly in the context of previous approaches to treatment of narcotics addicts, including Dr. Nyswander's wide-ranging history as a doctor among addicts. It is also useful to first examine some of the present "solutions" to the problem—such as the increasingly modish civil commitment of addicts.

A Doctor Among the Addicts, in somewhat different and briefer form, first appeared in *The New Yorker* as *The Treatment of Patients*. I am grateful to William Shawn and *The New Yorker* for permission to use the material here.

Nat Hentoff

9

a doctor
among
the
addicts

I FIRST came to know Marie Nyswander in the early 1960's. Part of her work at that time was a program in store-front psychiatric treatment of addicts in East Harlem. The program was undertaken in connection with the East Harlem Protestant Parish Narcotics Office. She is no longer involved with that office or with the East Harlem Protestant Parish's other activities with addicts for reasons which will be examined in a later chapter.

During those years I would often see Marie on an East Harlem street corner, a lithe, gesticulating woman surrounded by a cluster of men, black, brown, swarthy, and fair. Hatless, her coat open, hand on hip, she would parry questions and arguments, occasionally throwing her head back and laughing. On those occasions, she was on her way to or from her "office" in a bleak apartment on the first floor of a rotting, clamorous tenement on East 103 Street.

On Tuesdays and Thursdays, from two to as many as ten or fifteen addicts would be waiting to see her. She assigned no regular appointment times because addicts in general are not attuned to keeping set schedules. As the Reverend Norman Eddy, then Executive Director of the East Harlem Protestant Parish Committee, put it: "They have appointments in their own culture which take precedence over appointments in the square culture."

Accordingly, the addicts, knowing that Dr. Nyswander was available twice a week, dropped by on those days when and if they felt like it. Then and now most drug addicts had been frustratingly resistant to all those forms of treatment, including psychotherapy, whose main goal has been to keep them from returning to drugs. By working in East Harlem, Dr. Nyswander set herself a further challenge because many "lower-class" patients, whatever their problems, are also considered poor prospects for psychotherapy in view of the wide differences in backgrounds and methods of communication between them and middle-class professionals.

But during the four years she was most active in "storefront psychiatry," not only did several hundred addicts come to see the "bug doctor," but many continued to return. This was before her research into methadone, and she did not achieve a spectacular record of rehabilitating addicts. Furthermore, some of her patients remained at least as disturbed as when they started seeing her. But she did create and maintain sturdy relationships with a surprisingly large number of her casual visitors. "Clearly," a local minister observed during that period, "she fills a need in the lives of many people here. They seek her out, and that flies in the face of what is often said about the 'typical,' passive addict who cannot be reached."

14

The addict population of East Harlem, including those who knew Dr. Nyswander only by reputation, was impressed because, first of all, she was available to them in their own neighborhood, instead of in an impersonal institution or in a disturbingly unfamiliar private office in a section of the city alien to them. It is being increasingly realized that the drug addict cannot be fully understood or realistically treated outside the context of his own subculture. "So little is known about the addict that makes any difference," Reverend Eddy has emphasized, "but we do know that much."

One East Harlem addict, a Negro in his late twenties, had been seeing Dr. Nyswander since she came to the neighborhood in 1960. "You know," he told me, "the first time we met, instead of us getting right into the usual thing about my early childhood and my family, she wanted to know more about what was going on in the neighborhood. It shook me up. So I took her on a tour and introduced her to the fellows. She wasn't a bit afraid. You can feel the fear in a lot of people who come up here."

"I'd never felt right before about someone crawling around in here," he grinned, pointing to his head, "but I figured, 'This one's for real. She doesn't mind starting way down and finding out where everything is at.' Then, after awhile, I found out she was helping me find out where *I* was at. She was too hip for me to put on. I tried, but she cut through all that crap. I'd been telling myself and everyone else all these lies, when all along, what I have is a severe case of narcissism. I'm going to do what I want to do. And that's where *I'm* at."

Dr. Nyswander's candor is a major reason for her high standing in the addict community. She is also admired for her unself-conscious ease in speaking the argot of her patients; and her quick, mordant wit is similar to that of many addicts. "It's hard for us to develop a relationship with any stranger," a young, somber Puerto Rican in East Harlem has pointed out. "And it's especially hard when he's a professional who represents something better than you and who uses words that are beyond you. You know, not many of us finished high school. And besides, the other doctors are so damn serious. So what can you do? You tell them what you figure they want to know, but you don't open up. Maybe that's why the other doctors seem to think we all have the same story. But she didn't put us all in one box. She sorted us out, because she got inside. I could walk in next door and just blow my top if I want to; and believe me, she could blow *her* top too. Or, I could just light up a couple of cigarettes and talk about anything. And she'd never turn her back on you. Even if she was on her, way home to take care of the roast, she'd stop and talk. Look, what it comes down to is I dig her because she swings. I mean she's alive. She's really alive."

Seymour Fiddle, a sociologist on the staff of the East Harlem Protestant Parish Narcotics Committee, is skeptical of most psychiatrists who have tried to cope with what he terms the dismal science of the twentieth century. "The addicts," he maintains, "have made a science—or perhaps I should say an art—of guaranteeing their own failure." While he considered Dr. Nyswander insufficiently oriented in his own specialty, Mr. Fiddle did exempt her from his general strictures concerning her profession.

"Marie compelled these addicts to respond to her as total human beings," Mr. Fiddle said of her years in East Harlem. "At first, it was a shock for them to meet someone like her in a culture in which middle-class people either avoid them or see them as part of an undifferentiated segment—the junky. They've been beaten by policemen, hounded by judges, betrayed by lawyers, wept over by social workers. And then, to have someone from a 'higher' class ask your opinion of a book or a movie was startling. Most of the other psychiatrists I've seen working with addicts treat them *only* as addicts, and that's degrading. But once you start treating them as human beings, they begin to feel they're human beings."

16

One afternoon a few years ago, Dr. Nyswander was speculating about the reasons for her rapport with so many addicts. A slim, attractive woman with blonde hair, hazel eyes, and a voice of many textures—from deep growls of exasperation to bright enthusiasm—she walked briskly along Second Avenue in East Harlem, counterpointing her swift flow of talk with forceful movements of her hands. "They think of me as hip. I don't know exactly what that means." She looked at me as if to ask my definition, laughed, and continued. "Except perhaps I am. Essentially, when you work with an addict, you have to make sure that you yourself don't have—without being aware of it—a need to be needed, a need to cure him, to be important to him. You have to be careful you're not writing a contract in which you want something back from him. In any case, he's not about to give it to you. You may think you're giving him a lot of help, but from his point of view, it's pretty meager. His own tremendous well of self-pity makes it seem like a drop in the bucket."

Dr. Nyswander waved at two young men leaning against a store window. "Also, I have no vested interest in their being off drugs. I like them whether they're on or off. I like them because they're not stereotyped. We middle-class people all look pretty much the same. We have pretty much the same anxieties, the same conflicts, the same upward mobility strivings. But people who, by reason of class, personality, or subculture, do not get on that middle-class escalator, sometimes develop a uniqueness that I find enormously rewarding. Many of them are originals. You read novels in which the characters are unique, and you enjoy that experience. Here they are, right up here in East Harlem, if you can cut through your own conformity." She was silent for half a block, and then said slowly, "Not that I'm sentimental about them. They can be very exasperating. But I don't make them feel guilty—I hope. They're continually provoking their families to add to their store of guilt, but they can't play that tune with me."

17

Dr. Nyswander turned east on 103 Street and stopped briefly in the Parish Narcotics Office for her keys. The panes in the hallway door of the building containing her office were broken. As she walked in, three small children raced by her into the street. She opened the four locks which guarded her office, and once inside, she pulled a long chain attached to a bare 100-watt bulb in the light fixture on the ceiling. Nondescript curtains of brown cotton hid the room's two windows which were barred and overlooked a cluttered alley. The same fabric had been used to cover a narrow cot. Two chairs, a desk, a filing cabinet, and several shelves completed the room's furnishings.

The first visitor to the tenement office that afternoon was a slight, dark-haired, exceedingly soft-spoken man in his early twenties. He wore a black leather jacket, black pants, black shoes, and black socks. His mood was of the same color. With him was his sister, a plump, amiable woman, three to four years older. The young man, born in Puerto Rico, had been in New York since 1948. His addiction began in 1955, and during the years since, he had been withdrawn from heroin at several hospitals. Always he had relapsed. Recently he served a three-year term for possession of narcotics. Now he wanted to commit himself to a state hospital for detoxification and rehabilitation.

Dr. Nyswander started to fill out the requisite papers, but stopped to offer him a cigarette. He refused, shaking his head weakly. "When did you have your last shot?" she asked.

"Last night."

"How many bags are you kicking?"

"Two five dollar bags a day," he said, and looked up at the light bulb. (A bag is a glassine envelope containing a mixture of heroin and milk sugar, with some baby powder and perhaps a little quinine added.)

"Well," Dr. Nyswander examined the elaborate form in front of her with distaste, "what occupation should we give?"

18

"His occupation," the young man's sister interrupted, "is walking alone in the streets."

"I'll put down 'surveyor,' huh?" Dr. Nyswander smiled at the addict. He was not amused and began to tell her about the various factory machines he was capable of operating. For a moment his face became animated in his pride of accomplishment.

"But," his voice was barely audible, "I haven't been able to get a job. I stay with the habit."

"He almost got married a few weeks ago," his sister volunteered.

"I'll hit you over the head," Dr. Nyswander smiled again, "if you get married with a habit."

Another addict patient came in, after knocking, with coffee for the doctor. "You know how you need dope," she said to the Puerto Rican sitting opposite her. "That's how I need coffee."

There was the sound of running in the corridor, a crash of glass, and a series of sharp cries. No one in the room took any notice. The doctor returned to the form. "They want to know what symptoms have been manifested during the current addiction."

The sister grimaced. "They should know by now."

"Tell me," Dr. Nyswander turned to the young man, "what were the happiest days of your life?"

He looked at her blankly. "I can't remember any."

"Doesn't that strike you as strange or unusual, that a young man can't remember any moments of pleasure?"

He half-grinned and stared back at her.

"Do you think maybe you feel too guilty? Do you think maybe you feel you don't deserve to remember any pleasure?"

"No."

"All you remember is misery?"

"It's so hard to remember anything," said the young man.

Dr. Nyswander finished filling out the form, and then

19

asked what had happened to a friend of his, an addict she had been treating six months ago.

"Last I heard, he was in Lexington."

"Gee," said the doctor, "he gave me a rough time last summer. I really like him and that's why I blow up when he does that. I wish he'd get on his feet because he has a lot to give."

The young man and his sister left. Dr. Nyswander, waiting for the next visitor, lit a cigarette. "I wonder if the rat's here today," she said looking down at the cracked linoleum. "He's a big one, and when he comes around, I get on this chair and I don't come down until he goes." She laughed. "Much to the delight of the patients. It's an awful thing to be intimidated by a rat, but there it is. Weaker adversaries I'll take on."

She frowned. "That young man," she looked at the door, "has been detoxified six times at Metropolitan Hospital alone. Now he wants to lock himself up for what may be as long as three years. He's tired of the hustling involved with getting the money for drugs. And he's in such despair."

Dr. Nyswander smoked and drummed her fingers on the desk. "He's one of the ones who doesn't say much when he comes, but some of the others will stay as long as you let them. In one sense, conversation just for the sake of conversation certainly has a limited value; but there are some things that can be communicated in that way. The main thing is to keep a relationship going. Actually, you see, my work here in East Harlem could be called pretherapy. Someone has to build a bridge between the addict's subculture and the outside world. Once we've established a relationship, I'm here when he's ready to cross the bridge. I can withdraw him, give him letters of reference for work, or do whatever it is he needs to start across.

"That's why I do things in this pretherapeutic relationship I wouldn't consider in strict psychotherapy. I have coffee with them, buy them a sandwich and, once, I paid the rent for one of them. Sometimes, this kind of relationship is sufficient in itself as a way of holding on to them until they're ready to get out of the subculture. In that sense, what I do here can be termed a form of therapy. Other addicts, after beginning here, need deeper therapy, and some do get to the point at which they can try it, whether with me or someone else."

There was a knock, and a tall, self-assured man of about thirty came in, carrying a tape recorder. He was preparing a series of programs on addiction for an FM network, and Dr. Nyswander had agreed to be interviewed. She is shy of interviews, even when taped, and she stiffened as the machine was being set up. Reaching in her purse, she put on a pair of dark glasses.

"Why do you specialize in addiction?" was the first question. Irritated, she lit a cigarette. "I'm always asked that, and often it's asked suspiciously. I don't mean you," she smiled thinly at the man from FM. "But with so many people, the question is posed as if they have to believe I started in this because of a personal problem in my family. Some even look quickly at the pupils of my eyes, and when I see that happening, I can't resist rolling up my sleeves." The tape had stopped. The interviewer tried for ten minutes to get the machine in operation again but failed. Chagrined, he left.

Dr. Nyswander sighed in relief and took off her glasses. She leaned back in her chair. "I suppose the answer to that inevitable question," she began, "must include my reasons for being an analyst in the first place. I have a strong feeling for the beauty and dignity of man. And somehow, I have a feeling for the joy experienced by others, or at least their capacity for joy, and their desire to be liberated from repression. I like to be in on the process of release if I can. That's what motivates me to treat addicts and my other patients.

"Unfortunately, many psychoanalysts reduce all of life to a jargon. A safe jargon. They won't depart from middle-class

21

customs and values. But analysis ought to *free* you. Free you to experience joy and tragedy on a higher level than the interpersonal family level of relating to mother, husband, wife, or children." She rose, and walked up and down the room. "Suppose a patient has finished his analysis. An analyst might say the man is now able to express his aggression. But for what? Has he been made into a little aggressive island only large enough to include his wife and children? I'd feel greatly disappointed if someone I considered I had analyzed found such a sterile solution for his life. Is this what there is to life? We still know so little about man's capacity for creativity, for experiencing beauty, for freedom of a degree we can't yet imagine. We have to keep going into the unknown.

"That's why," Dr. Nyswander sat on the desk and leaned forward, "drug addicts can be so fascinating. In one sense, some of those I know up here strike me as among the few comparatively free people I meet during the day. Of course, they have a compulsion; but their compulsion is to drugs, not to smiling when you don't mean it and entertaining the boss for what you're going to get from him. Except when he's scrounging for drugs, the addict's relationships are usually honest and direct. The reason he's often deceitful when going after drugs is not that deceit is a basic part of his personality. It's an outcropping of his guilt over his illness; and deceit is also superimposed upon him sociologically because he *can't* get his drugs honestly. But when he's not hustling, his reactions can be trusted. He's not 'refined' in the way that striving for upward mobility necessitates."

She stood up and brought her hand down hard on the desk. "Addiction cannot be reduced to a simple masochistic, mechanistic act. For some addicts, drugs may be a way of keeping alive whatever life and joy they can feel. Until they're able to experience joy directly, drugs may perform a kind of stemming action for them. And while drugs are stultifying, they may also function for some addicts as a way into a mystical experience. I don't mean that addicts in this country become addicted in a conscious attempt at mysticism. But the action of the drugs, combined with the fact that in our culture addicts are cut off from society, forces some of them into a compulsive mysticism. They talk about the clarity of feeling, the oneness of perception they experience when they're on."

"In India and throughout the East," Dr. Nyswander continued, "they've had their lotus eaters—their drug addicts —for centuries. They grow up with them, they feed them, and they consider the addict part of the whole community as a balance against the materialistic proclivities of their society. In some cultures, moreover, religious mystics are forbidden to involve themselves in the tensions and desires of ordinary life. They're supposed to just sit and think. But there's no room for a mystic here. The best we can offer a few people is the Institute for Advanced Study at Princeton.

"Addiction, therefore, becomes a reflection of failure. They have failed to find themselves without drugs, and in view of what the addict is forced to become in this country, they have failed in so many other ways. Here the addict is forced into the abyss. He is forced to look at something in himself that every man has in him but that few men have fully faced—the fear of basic, total failure. Yet once a man has been down as far as many addicts go, he has a rare chance to find his *own* way out. Confronting failure so nakedly can bring out an honesty you rarely find elsewhere in our society. Hasn't nearly every great religious leader and artist and writer gone through horror, agony, torture, and temptation? And after having been cut off from all the predatory, repressive factors in society, some of them have come out of that degree of despair with an ethic they follow, not because they've been told it's right, but because they've derived it from *themselves*."

She lit another cigarette, sat down, and emphasized, "I'm not saying that addicts are poets or religious searchers, but many do seek the same quality of feeling poets do. Most don't have the capacity to make the observations of poets, but they do feel an obligation to themselves of a sort that is not common to this society. They want to know how far they can soar, how far they can see. And whether an addict does succeed in finding his own voice or not, he has at least looked his failure so fully in the face that he can't again really rationalize anything he does. Oh, he tries, and sometimes, when he's put on the defensive, he seems to do it effectively. But it's not a lifelong rationalization. For example, when an addict does develop the strength to stay off drugs and returns to society, he does not, so far as I have been able to determine, accept a dishonest way of life for himself. I've known a boy who's been off for two years. He's back in college, but he's no ordinary student. He's conforming to the demands of his school work, to be sure, but at the same time, he has his own unmistakable individuality. And I know former addicts in East Harlem who have also stayed free of the traps in which most of us are caught. Their humor, their perceptiveness continue to be uniquely their own."

"An addict confronting his reality existentially," Dr. Nyswander went on, "is different from the man who commutes on the train, drinks too much, sleeps with call girls at conventions or with his neighbor's wife. I wonder which of those two kinds of experience is more apt to lead a man to discover the truth about himself. It seems to me that the average person making his way successfully in America must feel very shabby at the end of the day because of the compromises, half-truths, withheld statements, and reactions forced on him by the compulsion to make it. And how great his despair must be when he realizes the $75,000 home and the two cars don't bring him any joy! Perhaps for many people alcohol and tranquilizers and barbiturates are serving the function of keeping a little joy alive, of giving life some meaning."

"You know," Dr. Nyswander smiled, "it's too bad

24

Americans aren't allowed to choose between hashish, on the one hand, and tranquilizers or alcohol on the other. Hashish is not addicting, relieves anxiety without subsequent depression, and is tremendously effective in relaxing the muscles. It may well be the best relaxing agent the world has ever known. And as it happens, the opiates—if social and legal pressures didn't so change the situation that terribly destructive elements enter into opiate addiction—are less mentally and physically debilitating than barbiturates, tranquilizers, and alcohol. There is no evidence that heroin causes mental deterioration, for instance, even after an addiction as long as fifty years. Although addicts neglect their bodies, and as a result, may appear emaciated or have rotting teeth, they're a surprisingly healthy lot. And not only are opiates cleaner, but they can, as I said, lead in some cases to greater clarity of vision and experience."

She began to laugh. "I'm not speaking out of experience. I can't ever imagine taking drugs, and I'm not a mystic. Nor certainly am I advocating that addicts remain addicted. Anyone who wants to should get off, and some addicts probably will if they're given a free choice. I mean if their addiction isn't stimulated by deprivation, as it is in this country. For one thing, there are marginal effects, such as diminished sexual pleasure, which may lead an addict to decide to get off. And fundamentally, there is something in man that desires that other kind of freedom—the freedom from *having* to do or take anything.

"Drugs can't be an end in themselves; or rather, I'd like them not to be. But there's more than one impetus for giving up drugs. You can give them up out of misery, as the boy who was here earlier this afternoon is apparently trying to do. But that kind of decision comes from total despair, not from health. You may also, however, get to the point at which you can relinquish drugs because you've found your own voice and can maintain it without help. It's *that* way I want for those patients who decide for themselves that they want to get off."

A short, wiry Irish boy of about eighteen knocked and came in. "Sit down, Billy," said Dr. Nyswander. "I expect you can contribute to this discussion. We were talking about reasons for staying off." The boy smiled, sat down, cocked his head, and listened. "The motivation has to be strong and from the inside," Dr. Nyswander continued, "because the pulls in the other direction are powerful and complex."

She looked at the cigarette in her hand. "I was off this for eight months last year, and I learned something while I was trying to stop smoking. The craving for cigarettes exists as an entity, separate from pleasure. Nor did the craving diminish with time. After six months, I'd still have dreams in which I'd surreptitiously cop a cigarette. Holy cow, if it's this hard to stop smoking, think what it must be to stop taking a drug such as heroin—a drug that satisfies man's most basic motivations. The addict on drugs is replete. He feels sexually satisfied, his stomach feels full, and he doesn't have to cope with aggressive strivings."

"And then," she looked at Billy, who was gazing at the ceiling, "there's the problem of tolerance. Once addicted to an opiate or its synthetic equivalents, the addict builds up a tolerance to the drug, requiring larger amounts to keep his body in balance and to prevent withdrawal symptoms. In other words, through the use of drugs, a new biological dependency such as thirst or hunger has been created."

Dr. Nyswander put out her cigarette and glared at it. "There's so much we don't know about addiction. There's been so little research yet, and we need a vast reservoir of information because the problem has so many basic components. You always have to look inward to see if you're missing an area of knowledge that keeps you from bringing everything you can to the subject.

"The reason we've learned so little, of course, is that for more than fifty years, the American medical profession has largely abandoned the drug addict. Because of the laws and the way they're administered, we've turned him over to the criminals. As a result, we're not even sure what kinds of addicts we've got here. British experts, for example, describe the addict as one who is normal on drugs, and that may be the definition of those who are true addicts. Off drugs, they may manifest severe character disorders, but they can function more or less normally while they're on. But in this country, we're confronted with the phenomenon of the law-produced addict who may well be sociologically hooked, and not a 'true' addict at all."

She looked at Billy.

"You don't mean me?"

"Yes, sir," said Dr. Nyswander emphatically. "You're a nonaddict addict."

Billy shook his head slowly. "I never thought of myself as a nonaddict addict. It's very disappointing."

"You didn't make it. Sorry. You have no reason for drugs. You're not that afraid of aggression, and whatever problems you have in that area, you could have mastered for yourself or gone to an analyst for help in handling them. You've got girls, humor, friends, a future, a past. And you're a hell of a good musician."

"So why am I using drugs?"

"As long as it's 'smart,' as long as it's against the law, young people like you will become attracted to drugs as an adolescent way of rebelling and also of exploring life. And then, if the drug you choose is, let's say heroin, a pharmacological action takes over and you're saddled with a thing that doesn't help you with your central problems. Not that it makes it any easier for you to get off even if you're not a 'true' addict."

"But," Dr. Nyswander ran a hand through her hair, "so long as we have our present laws, we're going to keep on having accidental addicts. And we're not going to be able to focus on the really interesting problems in addiction. Why is the true addict normal on drugs? Where does morphine mediate hunger, sex, and aggression? Where in the central nervous system are drugs absorbed and tolerated? There's some indication that a person who is psychotic or has had a lobotomy can't become addicted, but we don't know what has to be intact in the brain before addiction is possible. In what part of the unconscious, if any, does addiction come to play? These are some of the problems I want to study, not the sociology of the addict. These are questions with broader implications for man and his functioning than for the problem of addiction alone. But I can't get at them yet because the priority is to change the laws and to find ways to rehabilitate the addicts, accidental and otherwise, we now have."

Dr. Nyswander indicated it was time for Billy's session to start. At the door, she said, "The present situation is so damn senseless and can so often be tragic. Wait, someone put it more accurately: 'The American narcotics problem is an artificial tragedy with real victims.' "

THIS artificial American tragedy began with the enactment in 1914 of the Harrison Act, a regulatory and revenue
measure aimed at controlling the production and distribution
of narcotics, with the particular goal of limiting their avail-
ability to medical and scientific use. A combination of factors
in the last half of the nineteenth century had led to an
accelerating number of addicts among the populace, and
the Harrison Act was a product of the resultant alarm.

The cultivation of the opium poppy, *Papaver somniferum*,
for nepenthean and medical purposes, has been traced at
least as far back as the Sumerians, who by 7000 B.C. had
developed an ideogram, "the plant of joy," for the flower.

Opium was also part of the pharmacological knowledge of the Egyptians, Persians, Greeks, and Romans. It eventually spread to India, and by the ninth century A.D., Arab traders had introduced the poppies to China. In China, opium was usually taken orally or was smoked. Opium smoking was introduced to the United States in the mid-1800's when sizable numbers of Chinese began arriving.

Much more conducive to eventual widespread addiction here was the isolation in 1805 by F. W. Sertürner, a German pharmacist, of morphine, an active ingredient of opium. During the next thirty years, narcotine, papaverine, codeine, and other alkaloids derived from opium were discovered. The hypodermic needle had meanwhile been invented in Edinburgh in 1853, and the injection of morphine and other narcotics became common. During the American Civil War, narcotics were so generally used to ease the pain of the wounded that addiction became known as the "army disease."

The most pervasive cause of addiction in the nineteenth century was the generous inclusion of narcotics in patent medicines and other curatives. In her book, *The Drug Addict as a Patient*, published by Grune and Stratton in 1956, Dr. Nyswander has pointed out: "Before the addictive power of opium and other drugs was recognized, at least a million people in this country were exposed to addiction through patent medicines and physicians' prescriptions. Because of the soothing and analgesic properties of opium and its derivatives, these drugs were used indiscriminately to relieve everything from simple headache to angina pectoris. Various remedies with a narcotic content of 5 to 10 percent were sold without restraint over the counters of pharmacies all over the country. Through such wonder-working medicaments as Mrs. Winslow's Soothing Syrup, Dr. Cole's Catarrh Cure, and Perkins' Diarrhea Mixture, incredible amounts of opium, morphine, codeine, and cocaine were spooned into children as well as adults. Every well-equipped home had a rosewood chest, counterpart of the present day medicine cabinet, with its ball of opium and its bottle of paregoric."

By the late nineteenth century, there had been an appalled awakening, and alarmed talk began about the proliferation of "dope fiends" among the citizenry. (One Sears, Roebuck and Company catalogue announced Sears' Cure for the Opium and Morphine Habit. Sent in a plain envelope, the Cure was to be given without the addict's knowledge or cooperation.) Adding to the confusion was the isolation of heroin in 1898. This synthetic alkaloid, made from opium or morphine, was at first considered to be a non-addicting substitute for morphine and was substituted for the latter drug in tonics and cough medicines. Twelve years went by before the majority of physicians became aware that heroin, which is three to four times stronger than morphine, was indeed addicting.

In 1912, the United States took the lead in organizing the Hague Opium Convention in an attempt to establish international regulation of opium traffic. The delegates agreed to control domestic sale, use, production, and transfer of opiates and cocaine. Two years later, as part of this country's compliance with the terms of the Hague Convention, Congress passed the Harrison Act. It required that all legitimate handlers of narcotic drugs be registered and that a special excise tax be paid in connection with all transactions in drugs. Only physicians, in the course of their professional practice, could now prescribe these drugs.

Until the Harrison Act, the only effective control on drug traffic in America had been the prohibition of opium smoking. As late as 1913, addicts could buy morphine, for example, in a retail drugstore for about sixty cents for sixty grains when sold in the original bottles or in large portions. Doctors had been completely free to treat addicts and could prescribe a permanent regimen of drugs if withdrawal appeared too difficult or impossible. Initially there was no

31

indication that the Harrison Act would affect a physician's right to continue treating addicts according to his own best judgment.

Since 1914, this Act has been the foundation of American law enforcement of the drug traffic. As Rufus King, a lawyer with a particular interest in the narcotics problem, has observed, the Harrison Act "is not a forthright criminal statute, but rather a regulatory measure in the ill-tailored guise of a federal revenue enactment." Enforcement of the Act was first made the responsibility of the Bureau of Internal Revenue, was then shifted to the Bureau of Prohibition, and since 1930, has been the concern of the present Bureau of Narcotics in the Treasury Department.

In *The Drug Addict as a Patient*, Dr. Nyswander has described the transformation of the Harrison Act into a rigid program for the prevention of addiction, administered not by doctors but by law enforcement officials. "Federal agents," she notes, "were of necessity empowered to investigate and prosecute violations. There is no gainsaying the fact that there were numerous loopholes in the original Act—loopholes that had to be plugged to insure enforcement. But, upheld by Supreme Court decisions, the Bureau extended its activities until it assumed control of the domestic narcotic traffic and of medical treatment of addiction as well. Severe enforcement procedures were put into effect. Many physicians were imprisoned for administering to their patients. . . . When the legislators and enforcement officers ignored the terrible needs imposed on the addict by his disease, his one alternative was to turn to the underworld for relief."

Actually, the Supreme Court's role in the government's assumption of power over all aspects of narcotic control and administration has not been nearly so definitive as Federal enforcement officers have sometimes implied. In the early 1920's, the Court did uphold convictions of doctors who were clearly abusing their right to administer drugs by selling huge numbers of prescriptions to addicts. These doctors were not treating patients, but were simply selling drugs to all comers. In one such case (*United States* v. *Behrman*) in 1922, a majority of the court upheld the indictment of a doctor who had given an addict, in the course of one visit and for whatever use the addict chose, 360 grams of morphine, 210 grams of cocaine, and 150 grains of heroin.

Armed with the Behrman decision, the Narcotics Bureau launched what Rufus King has termed "a reign of terror." In his article, *Laws and Enforcement Policies*, in a symposium on narcotics for the Winter, 1957, edition of *Law and Contemporary Problems*, published by Duke University School of Law, King wrote: "Doctors were bullied and threatened, and those who were adamant went to prison. Any prescribing for an addict, unless he had some other ailment that called for narcotization, was likely to mean trouble with the Treasury agents. The addict-patient vanished; the addict-criminal emerged in his place. Instead of policing a small domain of petty stamp-tax chiselers, the Narcotics Division expanded its activities until it was swelling our prison population with thousands of felony convictions each year."

The Behrman decision was not the Supreme Court's last word on the subject. In a subsequent case in 1925, Dr. Charles O. Linder had been charged with having sold an addict-informer one tablet of morphine and three tablets of cocaine for self-administration. In its unanimous decision vindicating Linder, the Supreme Court made clear that the Harrison Act "says nothing of 'addicts' and does not undertake to prescribe methods for their medical treatment. They are diseased and proper subjects for such treatment."

Nine years later, the Circuit Court of Appeals of the Tenth Circuit applied the rule of the Linder case in *Strader* v. *United States*. In reversing the conviction of a doctor who had given an addict morphine, the Circuit Court declared that a physician was not precluded "from giving an addict a moderate amount of drugs in order to relieve a condition incident to addiction, if the physician acts in good faith and in accord with fair medical standards."

The Linder decision—and its application in the Strader case—had come too late. By 1925, as Rufus King has observed, the pattern had been set. "The trick," King wrote in the 1957 symposium, "had worked. The doctors had withdrawn, and they never permitted the addict to reapproach them. The peddler had taken over, and his profits soared as enforcement efforts reduced his competition and drove his customers ever deeper into the underworld, where they were easy prey. It is significant that the present-day regulation of the Narcotics Bureau advising doctors of their rights in dealing with addicts blithely ignores what the Supreme Court said in the Linder case. . . ."

Even if most doctors had not already been frightened off by 1925, there is a catch in the safeguards for physicians outlined in the Linder, Strader, and similar court decisions. The catch was explained by Judge Morris Ploscowe in the *Interim and Final Reports of the Joint Committee of the American Bar Association and the American Medical Association on Narcotic Drugs* (published as part of *Drug Addiction: Crime or Disease?* in 1961 by the Indiana University Press.) "A physician," Judge Ploscowe wrote, "who treats and/or prescribes drugs for an addict patient in good faith according to medical standards will be protected from a conviction. But his good faith and adherence to medical standards can only be determined *after a trial*. The issue of whether the doctor acted in good faith and adhered to proper medical standards must be decided by a judge or a jury. If the judge or jury decide against the physician, the latter may be sent to prison or deprived of his license to practice medicine."

"The physician," Judge Ploscowe continued, "has no way of knowing *before* he attempts to treat, and/or prescribe drugs to an addict, whether his activities will be condemned or condoned. He does not have any criteria or standards to guide him in dealing with drug addicts, since what constitutes bona fide medical practice and good faith depends upon the facts and circumstances of each case."

American doctors may finally be given a set of guidelines in this heavily mined area. The President's Advisory Commission on Narcotic and Drug Abuse has asked the American Medical Association and the National Research Council "to submit definitive statements as to what constitutes legitimate medical treatment of an addict, both in and out of institutions." Until such criteria are established and until they stand up in court, most American doctors will continue to refuse to treat addicts in private practice. The consensus of the profession is in agreement with the prudent counsel of Professors Shartel and Plant of the University of Michigan in their 1959 text, *The Law of Medical Practice*: "About the only safe courses open to him (the doctor) are to refuse to deal with the addict or to see that he is hospitalized in order to cure his drug habit."

A corollary of the abandonment of the addict by the medical profession is underlined by Dr. Theodore Rosenthal, former Narcotics Coordinator for the City of New York: "For two generations, American medical schools have lost all interest in dealing with the problem. The average medical student goes through medical school, internship, and residency —and I include those in Grade A schools and hospitals— and by the time he gets into private practice, he hasn't learned a single, solitary damn thing about addiction. When a sick addict knocks on his door looking for help, he knows only one thing—kick him the hell out!"

As private medical help became unavailable to addicts as a result of the way the Harrison Act was being administered, hospitals, once open to addicts desiring withdrawal, also finally refused to admit them. First of all, it became clear to hospital personnel that many volunteers for detoxification were motivated mostly by the temporary disappearance of their outside sources of drugs. In the hospital, they knew they'd be given drugs during the initial stages of withdrawal, and any relief was better than none. As the amount of drugs was reduced in the course of withdrawal, the addict usually left the hospital and was not seen again. Hospital administrators decided they had too many "legitimate" patients to care for without also having to operate a revolving-door sanctuary for addicts.

Futhermore, there was an increasing incidence of addicts smuggling drugs into hospitals, bribing attendants to get a supply, and sometimes physically forcing nurses to open narcotics cabinets. Also, hospitals became wary of accepting addicts because federal agents would occasionally confiscate hospital records, and on the basis of those records, the hospital as well as the patient could be prosecuted for alleged violations of the Harrison Act.

During the past few years, hospitals have been gradually opening again to addicts who apply voluntarily or are committed for detoxification. A limited number of beds for such patients is becoming available in more and more cities; but the addict who does not want to be institutionalized or who is not ready for rehabilitative treatment still has very few places to go for help except for those hospitals involved in the methadone project in New York City (see Chapter 9).

Between 1919 and 1924, more than forty American cities did experiment in providing aid to addicts through clinics which dispensed low-cost drugs. As a result of the American Medical Association's determined opposition to ambulatory treatment of addicts and the Treasury Department's own decidedly negative view of the clinics, all were eventually closed by threat of federal prosecution. In an interview in the periodical, *Modern Medicine*, in 1957, Dr. Nyswander admitted that poor planning and confused administration had led to the failure of the New York City clinic which opened in April, 1919, and closed in January of the next year. There were, however, several outstanding clinics elsewhere in the country, and of these, Dr. Nyswander observed: "All reports showed they would be successful, but the narcotic agents arbitrarily closed them before definitive problems could be worked out. Fortunately, the medical libraries contain a book by two public health people, *The Opium Problem*, by Terry and Pellens. This book contains the medical reports of the clinics and is vastly interesting reading. It indicates that, if the clinics had been continued, addiction today would be a simple medical problem and not the complicated sociologic problem it has turned out to be."

With clinics closed and doctors intimidated, the Federal Bureau of Narcotics was comparatively free to test its theory that the most effective way of curbing and preventing addiction was to increase the penalties for narcotics violations, and over the years the Bureau's program has been furthered by increasingly harsh federal and state legislation. Gradually, loopholes in the Harrison Act were filled in, and in 1925 the production or importation of heroin was prohibited by law, while a few years later unauthorized possession of narcotic drugs became explicity illegal. In 1956, Congress passed the Narcotic Control Act, which raised minimum sentences for drug violations and denied judges the power to permit probation or parole in many cases of narcotics-law violations.

At the White House Conference on Narcotic and Drug Abuse in September, 1962, James V. Bennett, then Director of the United States Bureau of Prisons, described the narcotics offenders under his care: "It is . . . extremely difficult to get this group to participate in our rehabilitative program. Few of them will wholeheartedly undertake a course of academic or trade training, they are indifferent members of our self-improvement classes and show little interest in any of the opportunities that are open to them. That, of course, is due

37

largely to the fact that we can provide no incentive for them. . . . They are doing what in prison parlance is called 'flat time'—a sentence without hope of parole or remission no matter how hard they may try to better themselves. Naturally, they look upon their institutional service as nothing but a trail of dead years. The consequence is that when their discharge finally comes, many leave little better than when they entered. In fact, some of them may be worse because whatever skills and industrial contacts they may have had have been lost. Even those who serve the shortest possible sentence for sale or transportation of drugs reenter a completely changed world. They are devoid of friends or relatives and they are feared, shunned, and discriminated against on every hand. Is it any wonder so many return to the only thing they know that will permit a brief escape?"

The states have gone along with the punitive approach of the federal government. As William Butler Eldridge demonstrates in *Narcotics and the Law* (American Bar Foundation, 1962), there has been an "almost unanimous trend toward increasing the severity of penalties in all the states. Maximum sentences of forty or more years as well as an increasing number of life sentences are liberally sprinkled through the provisions. Death penalties have been added for sales to minors. Nearly half of the states have some limitation on suspension, probation, or parole, which applies specifically to narcotics violations. . . . Despite the dearth of really conclusive evidence of the effect of severe repressive laws . . . the statutes consistently appear to reflect the idea that severity and severity alone can cope with the problem."

Some states have even tried to make addiction itself— as distinct from illegal possession, sale, or transfer of narcotics —a crime. In June, 1962, the Supreme Court decided that it was unconstitutional to make it a criminal offense to "be addicted to the use of narcotics." The case involved a California law under which an addict was automatically regarded as a criminal. No other law need have been broken. The Court declared: "It is unlikely that any State at this moment in history would attempt to make it a criminal offense for a person to be mentally ill, or a leper, or to be afflicted with a venereal disease. A State might determine that the general health and welfare required that the victims of these and other human afflictions be dealt with by compulsory treatment, involving quarantine, confinement, or sequestration. But, in the light of contemporary human knowledge, a law which made a criminal offense of such a disease would doubtless be universally thought to be an infliction of cruel and unusual punishment in violation of the Eighth and Fourteenth Amendments. We cannot but consider the statute before us as of the same category."

To the addict, the Court's decision is of small practical comfort. Once he is in possession of the drug to which he is addicted, he becomes a criminal anyway and is subject to the severe state and federal laws. Those laws, moreover, fail to differentiate sufficiently—and often, not at all—between nonaddicted major jobbers in the drug traffic and small-time addict-pushers. At one time or another, most addicts turn to selling to get enough money for their drugs, but most of the laws fall as heavily on them as on those to whom traffic in drugs is only a business.

A recurring motif in Dr. Nyswander's indictment of the punitive approach is that it has been responsible for the creation of a distinct addict subculture. An exact census of that subculture is extremely difficult to determine. It is clear that there was a decrease between 1938 and 1945 because it was virtually impossible in those years to smuggle heroin in from abroad. Since the mid-1940's there has been a decided upsurge, but standards of record-keeping throughout the country are so contradictory that no one really knows how many addicts there are. In the fall of 1962, an Ad Hoc Panel on Drug Abuse reported to the President that "the discrepancies between Federal, State, and local enforcement agencies are so great in some instances (more than 100 percent) that the Panel prefers not to make any numerical estimates at this time."

"By my criteria," says Dr. Nyswander, "the problem of addiction has assumed epidemic proportions. And it's important to remember that the drug addict before 1914 had little or no involvement with criminal activity. He carried on his job and maintained his home and family life. His illness did not inflict injury on anyone other than himself. He considered himself and was considered by others to be grappling with a definite and difficult problem and he expected to obtain treatment in a legitimate manner. Overnight, at least a million sick citizens were turned from sick people into criminals virtually by a wave of the legislative wand."

In her campaign to return the treatment of addicts to doctors and to dissolve the stereotype of the addict common among many in the medical profession as well as among laymen, Dr. Nyswander wrote *The Drug Addict as a Patient* in 1956. The book's intent was to demonstrate to general practitioners, psychiatrists, and hospital personnel that the addict, although often exceedingly resistant to treatment, could be dealt with by doctors willing to acquire a basic knowledge of addiction. No book of its kind had been published since the radical alteration of the narcotics problem in this country following the passage and implementation of the Harrison Act.

In 1957, Dr. Nyswander received a letter from Professor Dr. Joh. Booij of Amsterdam. As the editor of the *Folia Psychiatrica, Neurologica et Neurochirurgica Neerlandica*, Dr. Booij was about to review her book. He was troubled, however, at the possibility that he had not fully understood one of her themes. "From your book," he wrote, "I got the impression that in the U.S.A. these addicts are not treated like patients, but are taken in prison. Is that right? I am quite astonished to become aware of this. How is it possible, that these patients are taken in prison!"

Dr. Nyswander recalls Dr. Booij's astonishment with mordant exasperation at the American way of dealing with drug addiction. "How is it possible indeed? It's small wonder he couldn't quite believe what he was reading. This country has the harshest laws and, at the same time, the worst narcotic problem of any country in the world—and the most complicated. We've actually legislated into existence different kinds of addicts. They've all been thrown into a stew with diamonds and dirt and everything all rolled into one."

"Before the Harrison Act," Dr. Nyswander continued, "women addicts outnumbered men two to one. That ratio has been reversed. Before 1914, the addict population was much more likely to include the medically addicted and adults from the middle class. Now the majority of addicts are from working-class backgrounds, inhabitants of urban slums, and members of minority groups. And they're younger. America is the only country in the world with a large and growing quantity of adolescent addicts.

"The reason is that adolescents—by the nature of the beast—fight authority. Thoughout the world, adolescents are like a sensitive minority group waiting to be misunderstood and attacked. Traditionally, their criticism of the adult world has been acted out in student riots and radical political activities. Here, although there has been a recent growth in political activity by the young, the target of many continues to be the puritanism that remains in this country. Therefore, for some adolescents, addiction becomes the most tempting and the most rationalized of all revolts. That's why adolescents are so difficult to treat. A nineteen-year-old once told me an addict in his twenties had tried to persuade him to get off drugs. '*He* can talk,' the adolescent said. 'He's had years of it. I'm supposed to kick and I've only been on drugs two years. I'm being gypped.'"

"For some of them," she added, "getting on drugs becomes a way of stating their independence. These adolescents experience a kick out of the sense of identity they feel from being in revolt. Accordingly, at this point in their lives, they have very little motivation to be 'rehabilitated.' Whatever fear this kind of adolescent has he covers up, sometimes even from himself. If he feels he has to, he spits in the judge's face to show how brave and right he is. There are more adolescent addicts every year. Many kids who used to belong to fighting gangs have switched to drugs."

In addition to helping create a particularly refractory group of adolescent addicts, the punitive approach to drug addiction has also caused complications in the very nature of the drugs which addicts use. One veteran heroin addict told Dr. Nyswander a few years ago, "I can't understand why any kid would *want* to get on these days. There's nothing in the shots any more."

To increase the profits, entrepreneurs have increasingly cut heroin smuggled into the country until the average "bag" contains about 2 percent of the drug. The addict, furthermore, is always uncertain as to what he's actually buying. There is, after all, no one to set and enforce standards among the pushers and peddlers. The strengths in any given succession of bags may differ considerably; and as a result, serious accidents happen. An addict may inject more actual heroin during a shot than he realizes. When that happens, since he has become accustomed to a much weaker dosage, he may die. Deaths resulting from drug addiction—particularly death by overdose—used to be rare. In 1966, in New York City, there were over three hundred accidental deaths from narcotics addiction. In 1950, there were fifty-seven.

Another result of the uncertainty of each narcotics buy is that more addicts are developing mixed habits. "In the old days," Dr. Nyswander points out, "there were very few heroin addicts who also used barbiturates. Now more and more of them try various combinations of sleeping pills and the like to get the results that heroin alone used to provide. Because heroin has become harder to get and is increasingly diluted, I would say that more than 50 percent of today's addicts use other drugs to potentiate whatever heroin they can buy and to tide them over when no heroin is available. And these substitute drugs are more dangerous than heroin. They can alter judgment, cause mental deterioration, and can bring about convulsions."

"If, moreover, an addict with a mixed habit takes an overdose and is brought to the hospital, the doctor in the emergency room sometimes doesn't know what to do. If he could assume he was dealing with a straight heroin overdose, he could save the addict's life. But when he doesn't know what the addict has been taking, he may not have the diagnostic acumen and resources to find out in time how to bring him back."

"Despair," Dr. Nyswander spreads her hands in a gesture compounded of anger and impatience. "Despair has become the familiar of so many of them. Despair is always pulling them down, and that's why there's such a high suicide rate among addicts. We—I mean the doctors who feel as I do— have to get the addict coming to us instead of to the pushers; and the way to get most addicts out of their subculture is to give them drugs. We won't know all the directions in which we can go from there until we do a great deal more research on addicts who are getting drugs legally.

"As a matter of fact, we have had some knowledge of how addicts function when they don't have to worry about getting drugs. I'm not thinking of our methadone research at the moment. That's another story. I'm thinking of cases in which the addicts themselves have done the research, and we've been able to learn things from them we can't find out from addicts in institutions. It doesn't happen often, but once in awhile, one of the so-called vilest addicts in East

Harlem finds a doctor who gives him drugs or he gets an easy source from a friend. Under those conditions, he is likely to keep a job, maintain his family intact, and cut out his criminal activity. We see more of this kind of adjustment among middle-class and wealthy addicts who either have a medical disease which gives them a legal excuse for acquiring a regular supply or who discover a brave doctor. With these people, you see no social deterioration. I've yet to see a well-to-do addict arrested."

In recent years, there has been gradually increasing support for the inauguration of research projects which would treat addicts while they are able to maintain their drug habits legally. In 1954, the New York State Medical Association proposed to the American Medical Association that narcotics clinics be established under the auspices of the Federal Bureau of Narcotics. Addicts would be administered drugs at cost or without charge while attempts were being made to cure them. The next year, the New York Academy of Medicine advocated, as one method of treatment of addiction, that drugs be supplied to addicts at low cost under federal control. Whatever the percentage of cure, the Academy pointed out forcefully, at least this approach to the problem would take the profit out of illicit drug traffic.

In February, 1962, the Medical Society of the County of New York ruled that physicians "who participate in a properly controlled and supervised clinical research project for addicts on a noninstitutional basis would be deemed to be practicing ethical medicine." Such a clinical research project could include, if it seemed indicated, the prescribing of narcotics. The action was the first of its kind taken by any official medical society in the country since the passage of the Harrison Act.

The New York Academy of Medicine, in another report on drug addiction, in April, 1963, again recommended strongly that addicts come under medical supervision and that a doctor should be able to prescribe drugs legally if they appear in his clinical judgment to be necessary.

In June, 1964, the Advisory Council of Judges of the National Council on Crime and Delinquency declared— and this is still their position—that "the narcotic drug addict is a sick person, physically and psychologically, and as such is entitled to qualified medical attention just as are other sick people. As a sick person, the addict should receive whatever medical care he may need, as an outpatient of a clinic or private physician or, when necessary, in a hospital. . . . As the Supreme Court pointed out in *Linder* v. *United States*, the present law is interpreted—and should be so interpreted by the Narcotics Bureau or any other government agency—as allowing prescription of medicine, including narcotic drugs, 'for relief of conditions incident to addiction.' Despite this interpretation, the nature of administrative enforcement of the Harrison Act deters physicians from performing their ethical duties. Accordingly, the Advisory Council of Judges recommends that necessary action be taken, either by statute or by the appropriate bureaus and departments, to have the interpretation of the Harrison Act, as set forth in *Linder* v. *United States*, carried out administratively and the regulations of the Bureau of Narcotics amended to conform thereto."

In 1965, the General Board of the National Council of Churches urged, among other changes in the treatment of drug addicts, that doctors be given the full power "to determine the appropriate medical use of drugs in the treatment of addicts."

The weight of official medical opinion, however, is still against legalization of drugs and against ambulatory treatment of addicts. One standard argument, in lay as well as in medical circles, is that to provide some addicts with drugs would be an admission of defeat in terms of ultimately "curing" addicts. At one Washington conference on addiction in the early 1960's, Dr. James V. Lowry, then Assistant Surgeon

45

General of the United States, expressed this point of view to Dr. Nyswander. At the time, before she had begun research on methadone, she was on the staff of New York City's Metropolitan Hospital. She had pointed out to Lowry that many of her colleagues at the hospital agreed with her that under proper safeguards, addicts should be given drugs legally if their doctors so determined. Lowry shook his head. "What a depressing place that must be to work in," he said. "You've all given up."

"His reaction," Dr. Nyswander recalls, "seemed so irrelevant to me—aside from the fact that he was wrong. There was a great deal of enthusiasm among the medical personnel at Metropolitan as we learned more and more about addiction. And the basic point was, and is, that an addict's ability to withdraw from, and stay off, drugs cannot be set up as the only criterion of whether he is closer to being rehabilitated."

Dr. Nyswander has support for this view from Dr. Alfred Freedman, Chairman of the Department of Psychiatry at New York College-Metropolitan Hospital Center, where Dr. Nyswander is an assistant clinical professor of psychiatry, currently on leave of absence. At the White House Conference on Narcotics in September, 1962, Dr. Freedman noted that most current American programs for treating addicts centered on abstinence from drugs as a primary goal. He suggested instead that "social and medical rehabilitation and social integration are more meaningful goals in the treatment of addicts and that, in a rational approach to the problem of addiction, drug abstinence becomes one method along with many others of achieving such goals."

In other papers, Dr. Freedman has emphasized that for an as yet undetermined number of addicts, drug addiction may be a chronic disease and that those who are looking for a way to "cure" addicts completely should recognize that "by definition the duration of chronic illness is measured not in days, as is the case in acute illness, but in months and years, and recovery is seldom distinguished by a clear-cut end of symptoms." The success of most programs, however, is judged by the number of addicts who never again relapse. This method of evaluation, Dr. Freedman suggests, "may be eliminating a significant number who function in the community with variable success. They have brief relapses but manage to abandon the use of narcotics for a period of time by themselves or with medical aid. We do not know at the present time to what extent this is true, but it is not being measured and it should be. The weekend alcoholic is accepted in our society although the full-time alcoholic is considered a problem. It may well be that the concept of 'successful treatment' of narcotic addiction requires redefinition."

Another frequently heard argument against the legalization of drugs is that addiction is immoral and that anyone who helps sustain it is also committing an immoral act. Dr. David P. Ausubel, Professor of Education at the University of Illinois, has written extensively on addiction and one of his convictions is that "legalization would give drug addiction an unfortunate modicum of moral sanction that would encourage its spread among potential addicts. It is argued, of course, that the imposition of legal restrictions on socially disapproved commodities is self-defeating because they are not only circumvented by black-market operations but also give rise to all the undesirable correlates of a racket. By the same logic, however, one should advocate licensing of houses of prostitution by the health department."

Dr. Nyswander disagrees vigorously. "Giving drugs under medical control has nothing to do with right or wrong, good or bad. To make a moral question out of legalizing drugs as one method of treatment makes no sense to me. At the Public Health Service hospital for addicts in Lexington, Kentucky, they give drugs to addicts during research. Is it any more moral to do research in a prison than outside?

47

"The question which should be asked is: does giving an addict drugs help him get out of a situation in which he is stimulated to remain addicted by deprivation, and in the case of adolescents, by the continuing chance to be against authority? Does giving him drugs help him make his first steps back into society? To speak of providing drugs as a 'last resort' is inaccurate. It can be the first resort, the first way back, in a program of rehabilitation which has the addict's consent. But all the official programs keep insisting that the addict be off drugs before he can start being rehabilitated."

WHILE harsh federal and state punitive laws concerning narcotics addiction remain on the statute books, a burgeoning recent trend has been in the direction of providing alternatives to those laws for some addicts. This is the "civil commitment" approach under which certain addicts can voluntarily place themselves—or be placed under court order—in hospitals and other institutions intended to cure and rehabilitate them. Those accused of certain minor crimes can elect this civil commitment in lieu of prosecution. It is also possible in some states—and under a new federal law— for addicts to be civilly incarcerated even if they have committed no crime but are adjudged to be addicted.

The federal civil commitment law is the 1966 Narcotic Addict Rehabilitation Act. That bill also authorizes $15 million for each of two years for grants to the states to help them build and operate treatment centers for addicts. This approach—civil commitment and the building of more treatment centers for those committed—has been adopted in one form or another on the state level by California, Arkansas, Maryland, Illinois, and New York, among other states.

The New York State program went into effect on April 1, 1967. A Narcotic Addiction Control Commission was set up with an operating budget that could reach $400 million in the first three years. The funds are to provide facilities and staff for commitment, aftercare, and rehabilitation centers. Under the new law, anyone arrested and possibly addicted has to take a medical examination to determine whether he is, in fact, an addict. If he is convicted of a misdemeanor and has been shown to be an addict, the court has to remit the defendant to the custody of the Narcotic Addiction Control Commission. And, even if the addict has been acquitted of the misdemeanor charges, he may still be turned over to a civil hearing and committed for civil treatment up to three years. Furthermore, any prostitute who is an addict can be civilly committed for a maximum term of three years.

If an addict is convicted of a felony, the court has the discretion of sending him to a prison or to the Commission. Addicts convicted of crimes punishable by death or life imprisonment must be sent to prisons. Under another provision of the law, "anyone who in good faith believes a person is an addict" can institute proceedings—with legal safeguards, it is said, for the suspected addict—to have him civilly committed for a maximum three-year term of rehabilitation. To civil libertarians, myself included, the law is dangerous on civil liberties grounds alone.

"The basic proposition underlying it," says the New York Civil Liberties Union which is testing the statute, "is that addicts are dangerous to others. Because they are dangerous they must be removed from society and certified to places where they can inflict no harm. The fallacy in this is that in the absence of any other evidence, addiction, standing alone, is no proof of dangerousness. To deny a person liberty, to confine him for a period of up to three years, when he may not constitute any threat at all to society, should shock the conscience of anyone dedicated to freedom."

In their losing campaign against the new program in the New York State legislature, Senator Manfred Ohrenstein and Assemblyman Jerome Kretchmer emphasized: "The compulsory program isolates the addict like a leper. What we need is a medical program for the ambulatory treatment of addicts so they can function as productive members of society while still being treated for their illness." And Nathan Straus III, who has spent many years in research on addiction, predicted: "The simple expedient of confining the individual addict until he is no longer physiologically dependent on drugs can do little more for society than contain a single case for a few years. For the addict himself, it usually does nothing at all."

Dr. Nyswander agrees. "You can call it 'civil commitment,' " she says, "but it's a lockup program. And furthermore, if we've learned anything about addiction, we've learned that a medical program which is *not* acceptable to the patient will not work. In large part, the New York program was based on California's civil commitment laws. But what has happened in California? After one year of being released from civil commitment, 70 percent of those involved have returned to institutions; after two years, it's 80 percent; and after three years, 90 percent. So too, in New York State, after spending all these millions of dollars, we're very likely to find that all we've accomplished is to take three years of these people's lives.

"I hope we don't have to go through another thirty years

of failure to find out that civil commitment is not *the* answer either. After all this time, more and more people are beginning to admit that criminal commitment doesn't work. But the people, in and out of legislatures, who are supporting this 'new' approach don't seem to realize that civil commitment with medical treatment is still compulsory treatment, except for those relatively few addicts who will volunteer. We know that when an addict is sent to jail, one of the first things he will often do when he gets out is to take a shot of heroin so that he can feel like a human being again instead of an outcast who has been quarantined. An addict forced into a hospital under civil commitment is quite likely to do the same thing.

"It's easy enough to withdraw an addict from drugs. Many can be withdrawn at home. But then what happens? And if you've withdrawn him in a hospital, what will happen when he's released again if he has not *wanted* to stop using drugs by himself? My concern is that there will be a focusing of money and energy on civil commitment as the new cure-all for narcotics addiction. Certainly some addicts can be helped in a hospital. Some function well in treatment systems like Synanon, in which they're guided by a staff of former addicts and gradually assume authority on their own. But all the hospitals and all the Synanons in the country cannot meet the needs of all addicts.

"For addicts who are *not* ready to get off drugs, however, I do think our experience with methadone indicates that this drug can be an important means to rehabilitation. The advocates of civil commitment—those who say no rehabilitation is possible until the addict is absolutely drug-free—refuse to consider that we can find out more ways of motivating the addict toward rehabilitation if we are able to give him drugs while he tries to find his place in the world. Let the addict find out for himself whether he functions better on or off drugs.

"Suppose you run out of cigarettes at 11:30 at night.

You've still got a lot of work to do. You're tired; it's snowing; but you get your clothes on and start thinking where the nearest all-night delicatessen is. There's no possibility of your thinking about work at that point. Similarly, you can't ask most drug addicts to stop and consider what vocation they want to go into, or to evaluate anything, so long as their primary preoccupation is to get drugs. When an addict no longer has to worry compulsively about his source of supply, then he can concentrate on other things. At that point, rehabilitation can become a meaningful word. Of course, if an addict decides to go off drugs right now, you can get him into a program which doesn't take his need for drugs into account, and his prognosis may be good. But most addicts have not yet made that decision."

When asked how long she thinks it will be before being drug-free will no longer be considered the criterion as to whether an addict can be rehabilitated, Dr. Nyswander expresses some optimism. "In March, 1967, our methadone program was expanded in New York City under the recommendation of the city's medical evaluation panel. We will now have the funds to take in one thousand addicts this year. Despite the trend toward civil commitment, there *is* a definite change in the climate of opinion concerning the treatment of drug addiction. When my book came out in 1956, I was considered a heretic whose license should be taken away. Now I'm legitimate, though controversial. And look at the sources of support those of us are getting who believe that an addict doesn't necessarily have to be 'clean' to become a functioning member of the society."

She cites a lead editorial in the April 17, 1963, *Wall Street Journal*. Criticizing previous official approaches to addiction, the editorial pointed out that "rehabilitation and cure are not necessarily identical," and went on to recommend that "we should begin considering how physicians, under careful rules, can be allowed to treat these sick people as they do

53

others; and we can start searching for ways in which the tragic incurables can be put on sustaining doses that will keep them from desperate acts."

There was also, she adds, an editorial in the February 27, 1965, *New York Times*: "The best hope for smashing the illicit traffic in narcotics lies in the dispensing of drugs under medical controls—particularly at hospitals in the needy sections of the city, where physicians and psychiatrists can initiate well-rounded programs of medicine, counseling and therapy as a basis for helping addicts overcome their dependence on narcotics."

In recent years, as the changing climate has been making Dr. Nyswander appear to be less of a heretic, she has acted as a consultant to many of the programs concerning drug addiction in New York City, both municipal projects and those conducted by voluntary agencies. In 1959, for example, she was research committee chairman of the Mayor's Advisory Board on Narcotics Addiction, and in 1965 she was appointed by the city to set up units in a number of New York's teaching hospitals for further experiments with methadone.

Dr. Nyswander has considerable experience also in the treatment of medical men who have become addicted. Physician patients come to her from all over the country. Some are in legal difficulty because of their addiction, and others want to get off drugs for fear of imperiling their careers. Dr. Nyswander is accepted as an expert witness by the attorney general's office in cases concerned with addicted physicians. When a doctor has had his license to practice suspended because of his own drug problem, she is one of a group of approved physicians whom the addicted doctor can ask to give a prognosis of his case when he applies for the return of his license. She may also be asked to testify for him if he is up for sentencing on a narcotics charge.

"In either situation," she emphasizes, "I never testify for a doctor unless I have a secure feeling that he is seriously working on his problem. I do feel very sorry I can't put physicians on methadone, but unfortunately it's against the law for anyone to practice medicine if he is on drugs. I'm convinced, however, that a physician on methadone could function very well indeed. Why, we have people in our program who work in hospitals—imagine, a *hospital* hiring an addict! And others of our patients work in all kinds of sensitive, responsible jobs. But so far, physicians cannot be included in our program. I'm convinced, however, that the time will come when there'll be general agreement that an addict can be rehabilitated even if he is on a drug such as methadone. And then those physicians who cannot get off drugs before beginning their rehabilitation will have hope. It used to be that most addicts couldn't afford hope. Now those on the methadone program can."

MARIE has been the most visible figure in psychiatry working on addiction. No one in the country has stayed with the treatment aspects of the problem so long and so creatively." Making the comment was Dr. Charles Winick, a psychologist and expert on addiction. Because of that visibility, Dr. Nyswander has been besieged for years by calls for help.

A parent remembers having seen her name in the paper and telephones her about a son, or a doctor with little knowledge of addiction recalls an article of hers in a medical journal and sends her a patient. Hospitals, municipal and voluntary agencies, and the New York County Medical Society are among the other sources of the large number of telephone calls she receives.

And through the years, as her name has become more publicized, Dr. Nyswander has also heard from isolated doctors around the country who write her about the addicts they've treated. "Hearing from them," she says, "has strengthened me and has given me a lot of useful data. This is one tremendous learning process, and I can learn most from the widest possible spectrum of different experiences."

"Sometimes, however," Dr. Nyswander has observed, "I feel like some kind of information service. My name is given out like they hand out baksheesh in India. There are weeks when I get from five to twenty calls a night. Once, for example, there was a man who had just discovered his daughter was an addict. He had her chained to the bed. She was sick and vomiting. Over the phone—over the phone, mind you—I had to get him quieted down. Then I called a drug store to get some medicine over there. She may have still been chained to the bed the next day, but at least she wasn't sick. About an hour later, I got a call from a woman in East Harlem. Her husband is an addict, and he had just stolen the family television set. There wasn't anything I could do for her."

Dr. Nyswander's first venture into the problems of addiction took place in 1945 when, as a Navy doctor, she was stationed for a year at the United States Public Health Service Hospital in Lexington, Kentucky. The Lexington institution is one of two Public Health Service hospitals whose construction was authorized by Congress in 1929 as centers for the confinement and treatment of people who had committed offenses against federal narcotics laws. The hospital at Lexington was opened in 1935, and the other, in Fort Worth, Texas, in 1938. Both hospitals were also allowed to treat addicts who were willing to go there voluntarily for withdrawal and rehabilitation.

"The year I spent at Lexington," Dr. Nyswander recalls, "was the most miserable I'd ever known. Because of the way

I'd been raised, I was totally unequipped to cope with the attitudes which prevail in a prison, and that essentially is what Lexington is. I'd never had anything to do with addicts before, and when I left, I never wanted to see another one as long as I lived."

The contrast between this first experience with the addict in confinement and nearly everything she had previously known was indeed startling for the young physician. She had been born in Reno, Nevada, on March 13, 1919. On her mother's side, she came of pioneer stock, third-generation residents of Nevada who had originally emigrated from England and Australia. Marie Nyswander's mother remembers having been able to see from miles away the dust of the stage coach coming to make deliveries to her home. "That Western background," Marie Nyswander says, "was an important influence. The past is always with me."

Her father's family was German in origin, and many of the male members had been professors. James Nyswander, now retired, was a professor of mathematics at the University of Michigan for many years. Marie Nyswander's parents were divorced when she was two, and she was raised by her mother, Dorothy Bird Nyswander.

A woman of prodigious energy, Dorothy Nyswander acquired a master's degree in mathematics and a doctorate in psychology and did pioneering research work in public health on the state and then the national level. After World War II, she was appointed a professor at the University of California School of Public Health in Berkeley.

During the past decade Dorothy Nyswander became involved in public health activities abroad. "My mother," says Marie Nyswander with pride, "is an expert in finding out why a public health project is not being accepted by the people for whom it was designed. When such problems occurred she was called in to do the kind of research that should have been done before the project was started."

After working in the rural fastnesses of Turkey and in nearly every country in South America, Dorothy Nyswander spent three years in India for the Ford Foundation.

"I remember seeing her," says her daughter, "in New Delhi in January of 1963. She was in her mid-sixties, and there she was with her bedroll, climbing into a jeep to head somewhere away from civilization. She's totally fearless. I remember, when I was a child, we were once camping in the mountains above Yosemite National Park in California. All of a sudden, there was a grizzly bear. My mother went up to him, clapped her hands, told him to get away, and he did.

"She's still the same. When she was working overseas, she would fly little planes into jungle villages, had no qualms about getting dirty in the course of her work, and the only concession she made to her own safety was to carry a bottle of iodine from which she poured a drop or two into the muddy water used for drinking in remote areas.

"I guess you could say she's steeped in the ethic of the professional class; and when I was growing up, I was drilled in that concept of noblesse oblige—the privilege and obligation of being of service to others."

Her mother, Marie Nyswander claims, is much better known than she is in medical circles. "I'm frequently mistaken for her. I'll go to a meeting and someone will say, 'I didn't know you were so young. My goodness, how old were you when you did that pilot study on the public health aspects of school systems?' 'I was ten,' I'll say." The daughter is significantly different from her mother in her bent for working with individuals rather than on public health problems. "The kind of work my mother does is very exciting and important, but I've always been drawn to the beauty of a single human being's structure, which is not to be found in statistics or massive programs."

The drive for service which Dorothy Nyswander instilled in her daughter was coupled with an equally forceful proselytization for making the most of all her capacities—intellect, sensual pleasure, the aesthetic sense. "I remember her," says Marie Nyswander, "as a very feminine and attractive woman with great humor. She loved to see people happy—me in particular. There were never any bounds on me. I doubt if I ever sat through a meal at home. If I was too full of energy and wanted to play the piano or do something else, I'd just leave. I was very fortunate in the totality of the freedom I had as a child. By the time I was eight, I'd go off for days in the mountains and my mother wouldn't worry because she knew I was thoroughly trained in mountain climbing."

The girl was also allowed intellectual freedom. As she grew, she became absorbed by the conversation of such frequent weekend guests of her mother as anthropologists Ruth Benedict, Margaret Mead, and Cora Du Bois as well as a number of psychologists and psychoanalysts, including Max Wertheimer, one of the initiators of Gestalt psychology. "They'd sit around the fireplace," Marie Nyswander recalls, "talking about future research plans and trading ideas while I'd be under the piano, permitted to chip in my opinions whenever I wanted to."

Although born in Reno, Marie Nyswander started school in Berkeley, California, where her mother was finishing requirements for a Ph.D. When Dorothy Nyswander secured a teaching position at the University of Utah, the family moved to Salt Lake City. Bored in grammar school, which was part of the university, the girl spent hours in the biology, zoology, and psychology laboratories. She herself was often used as a subject for psychological experiments.

"It was marvelous," Marie Nyswander says, "being exposed to this background of science and also having the intellectual freedom to explore it at the same time as I had physical freedom. Freedom and mobility—those were the characteristics of *this* family!"

At fourteen, Marie Nyswander was discovered to have

tuberculosis. She spent a year at a sanatorium in Monrovia, California. Her reading there ranged from *The Magic Mountain* to John Strachey's *The Coming Struggle for Power*. On the jacket of the Strachey book was the address of a Los Angeles book store. One night she slipped out of the sanatorium and went to Los Angeles. In a dark street, she found the address, an old building. Inside, some eighteen old men sat around a table, discussing a book on anthropology. "I thought it was some kind of heaven," she remembers. "Those seedy-looking people were so involved in this heavy literature."

She had, in fact, come upon a branch of the Socialist Labor Party. She bought as many pamphlets as were available and returned to the sanatorium to question its director as to what happened to poor people with tuberculosis. He told her about crowded public hospitals with much less tempting food than she was getting, and she decided the only course for her was to become a revolutionary. She had her chance the summer she was released from the sanatorium.

"I had a car—my mother's—and although I never forgot it was a capitalistic car," Dr. Nyswander recalls, "I did use it for good causes that year. I distributed pamphlets; drove the people who were trying to organize the apricot pickers; and while on foot, I became rather expert in eluding the police who liked to try to run their horses into you." The young revolutionary had to move to New York where her mother had become involved in a research project. There she helped raise money for the Spanish Loyalists and distributed more pamphlets. Her inability, however, to stay within rigid patterns of dogma led to her dismissal from one radical group as a philosophical anarchist. She tried the Trotskyites, but they, too, thought her insufficiently manageable. "And so," Dr. Nyswander recalls, "I went to Sarah Lawrence."

The freedom at Sarah Lawrence seemed to Marie Nyswander to be an extension of her own home. "I was the first premedical student they'd had, and when it was necessary

—as in the courses I wanted in physical chemistry and advanced mathematics—they got teachers from the outside. When it came to psychology, they simply designed a whole course for me. I'd already learned so much from Mother and her friends that I was allowed by the college to study with Max Wertheimer at his home as part of my program."

Helen Lynd, who was teaching social philosophy at Sarah Lawrence, decided during Marie Nyswander's senior year that the girl was developing an almost fanatical attachment to science. She had a tendency to focus exclusively on the empirical and had small regard for anything that couldn't be subjected to scientific methodology. "Professor Lynd," Dr. Nyswander recalls, "called in John Storch, a metaphysician, to minister to me. We would sit under the trees and he would shake me to my roots. At first, I hated and fought him. It was terribly unnerving, learning that there were no absolutes, except within frameworks particular to each. Somehow I'd never thought in terms of those relative frameworks."

For a time at Sarah Lawrence, there was a conflict between Marie Nyswander's medical intentions and her passionate involvement with the piano. She had been studying the instrument since she was three and continued lessons while at Sarah Lawrence and later, through medical school. At the college, she was the resident pianist for students of German lieder. In the process, she learned the language and developed a continuing affection for the songs themselves.

"I had a yearning to be a pianist," Dr. Nyswander says, "but I couldn't have been content to be only a performer. If I had been able to create my own music, I might have decided differently. In any case, I must have really known all the time that I was going to become a doctor. Medicine is such a compelling drive that I doubt if any doctor does have an actual second choice. I'm not sure why it's so compelling. Service. Prestige. Security. Independence. It must be a constellation of certain needs within yourself. I remember thinking that above all, I would be independent and could go wherever I wanted to."

Having been admitted to all twenty medical schools to which she had applied, including Edinburgh, Marie Nyswander chose the Cornell University Medical College, which is affiliated with New York Hospital. She decided to become a surgeon, and her internship was at Meadowbrook Hospital in Hempstead, Long Island. Instead of concentrating on any one specialty, she had a "rotating" internship, covering surgery, obstetrics, orthopedics, contagious diseases, and other areas of medicine. Because it was wartime the staff was small and the work was grueling. "Night and day," she recalls, "we rushed through everything with hardly any sleep, no cigarettes (because of rationing), and never time to finish a meal. It was tremendously exciting. There were accidents every night, a lot of orthopedic surgery, and I also delivered hundreds of babies. It was a great, great internship."

In the fall of 1945, Dr. Nyswander went into the armed services as an orthopedic surgeon. The original plan had been for her to head one of the fifty-bed hospitals in China being operated by the United Nations Relief and Rehabilitation Administration. It was decided, however, that she was too young to be entrusted with that much responsibility. She had received her commission as a lieutenant junior grade in the Navy as a prerequisite for the UNRRA assignment, but the Navy itself had no provision for women doctors. Accordingly, Dr. Nyswander was transferred to the United States Public Health Service, which manned the marine hospitals. One of those institutions was the narcotics center in Lexington, Kentucky, half of which had been turned over to American servicemen who had been prisoners of war of the Japanese. The other half still housed drug addicts, both prisoners and volunteers. Although she did some surgical and psychiatric work with the returned servicemen, Dr. Nyswander spent most of that year with the drug addicts.

"When I arrived," Dr. Nyswander remembers, "I had no particular interest in the addicts as such. I had a medical job to do, and we did many different things—surgery, withdrawal, therapy, and parole evaluation. That last job," Dr. Nyswander says with unabated bitterness, "was horrible—being put in a position to say when another human being is going to get in the sun again. I couldn't think of anything that would make me say, 'No,' and I never did say, 'No.' "

Dr. Nyswander soon developed rapport with a number of the addicts. "The doctors were pleasant," she explains, "but they had their families. As for some of the other personnel, they soon began calling me addict-lover and nigger-lover, so there was no companionship there. But it did seem to me that the addicts were especially sensitive to my isolation. Here I was at twenty-six, the only woman doctor in a prison. In addition, I'd been spoiled by having been raised in a professional, liberal background. I was totally unprepared for that kind of constricting existence. It was often a case of the addicts cheering *me* up. Although they usually kept to the prison code of not informing on each other, they would inform on a patient who was giving me a rough time. Most of the Negro patients were particularly kind to me. They were encouraging, and they'd play jazz for me, something they usually did only for themselves. At night, they'd often sneak milk shakes into my room. They kept me going, asking nothing from me. They just gave, although there was no reason for them to."

Not all the addicts, however, treated the young doctor sympathetically. "I was mugged a few times by addicts looking for drugs, and once, a big, tough girl dragged me into a room, insisting I give her the key to the drug cabinet. I didn't have it so she roughed me up a little. It was frightening at times. The women were especially difficult. Occasionally they'd riot, and the guards would ask *me* to go over there and reason with them." One such mission was caused by a group of women prisoners setting fire to the curtains and mattresses in their dormitory. Dr. Nyswander, trembling with fear, walked into the maelstrom, offered the women cigarettes, talked to them, and eventually calmed them. "I can't tell you how I did it. Perhaps they were able to feel there was something in me, too, which resisted being in a prison. I was always breaking rules there without knowing it."

When Dr. Nyswander first arrived at Lexington, there were women who had not been allowed outside their own building for four years, except for a movie in the men's section once a week. "Vicariously," she recalls, "I got acute claustrophobia." Behind the women's building was a fenced-in yard, covered with weeds. Dr. Nyswander tried to get permission to convert it into an outdoor recreation area. Before the various levels of bureaucracy ruled on the plan, she was allowed to take the women patients for walks around the grounds on Sundays. A rigid rule prohibited the sending of "kites" (messages) to the male addicts. A couple of Dr. Nyswander's charges broke the rule, and the walks came to an end.

She continued to make plans for the rehabilitation of the backyard, but a psychopathic patient in an access of rage destroyed all her informal blueprints. An older doctor on the staff comforted Dr. Nyswander. "Marie, when you diagnose a patient as a psychopath, it figures she'll behave like one."

"It was a good lesson for me," Dr. Nyswander emphasizes. "I had thought that in their respect for me and in their reaction to my great desire to help them, they'd all act differently. I had to learn that patients' own needs and particular sicknesses determine what they do. You can't function well with addicts, for example, if you try to gratify your own needs through them. They have more pressing problems than satisfying you."

At one point in her lonely year at Lexington, Dr. Nyswander, particularly depressed because of racial discrimination by some of the personnel, thought of leaving. Her commanding officer said that she could ask for a transfer since she found conditions so difficult. "But," he went on, "this is your first job. If you begin your career in this way, how will you feel later about having made this kind of start?"

"That was what I needed," Dr. Nyswander observes. "The tears dried, I set my chin, and finished the year. To work out some of my hostilities and frustrations, however, I began punching a bag in the gym until my knuckles were black and blue. Playing the piano in the chapel also helped."

Of her last months at Lexington, Dr. Nyswander remembers with particular distaste an order from the commanding officer to join him for horseback riding on Sunday mornings. "He wanted company, but all I could think of was how appalling it was—how like being lord and lady of the manor—to go bounding over the prison grounds while the patients watched behind bars."

She remembers with more humor than discomfort another incident at Lexington—the only experience she has had with heroin. "It was part of the research that goes on there. The staff is used as a control group. They don't tell you what the drug is you've taken, but I assume it was heroin. I had one shot, administered by hypodermic needle, and I was sick. The research unit was in the bowels of the prison, and I had to walk past all the patients in their cells, through the grills, and across the courtyard to my room. I was staggering in my distress, and they somehow knew I'd had a shot. They thought it was very funny. I got to my room and vomited."

Dr. Nyswander was immensely relieved when her year at Lexington was over. "It had been awfully hard. I was a young girl with undefined needs to help people, and at the same time, I didn't know much about my own needs. Besides, dealing with addicts in a prison situation made me unable to comfort them. It was a circle of frustration. I never wanted to see another addict."

WHEN she resumed her training in New York, Dr. Nyswander confirmed a decision she had made during her internship on Long Island. "It had become clear there that I liked being the first assistant surgeon but that I hadn't much interest or real ability in terms of devoting all my professional time to surgery."

Her goal now was psychiatry and psychoanalysis. She enrolled in a three-year comprehensive course in psychoanalysis at New York Medical College.

After completing her residency, Dr. Nyswander continued with her analysis, and in 1950 started private practice. She was graduated from the Comprehensive Course in Psychoanalysis at New York Medical College, and became a Diplomate of the American Board of Psychiatry and Neurology. Dr. Nyswander had not yet included narcotics addiction among her primary interests. For several years, much of her energy was committed to the Postgraduate Center for Psychotherapy, a low-cost clinic which included research activities as well as training and therapeutic services. There she worked as a clinical director and senior supervising psychiatrist.

While at the Postgraduate Center, she was also involved for two years with the New York City Health Department in a project aimed at orienting pediatricians into the ways a psychiatrist would react to some of the pediatric and family problems they encountered. "I suspect," says Dr. Nyswander, "that I went into that experience without fully examining my motives. It may have been an attempt to follow in my mother's footsteps. I worked for awhile in the same Health Department district in which mother had done her research on the public health aspects of the school system, and her desk was still there. I finally pulled out of it. It wasn't the milieu for me, but it was a nice failure experience."

Concurrent with her private practice and her work at the Postgraduate Center, there was a gradual increase in Dr. Nyswander's concern with the problem of narcotics addiction. "When I came back from Lexington," she says, "I was surprised to find out how little most doctors knew about addiction." While in residency at Bellevue, she saw a doctor suddenly and totally cut off from all drugs a man addicted to barbiturates. At Lexington, Dr. Nyswander had learned to carefully withdraw addicts. One method was by decreasing doses of morphine, then codeine, and then thiamine along with sedatives so that the patient could rest at night. Another way was to stabilize the patient on morphine, and then to substitute methadone in gradually smaller amounts until it could be eliminated entirely. Patients addicted to barbiturates were withdrawn by gradually reducing the dosage of the barbiturate and eventually replacing the drug with chloral hydrates until the patient was able to sleep without any sedatives.

"Seeing 'cold turkey' being used at Bellevue," Dr. Nyswander recalls, "impelled me to protest. I was amazed to find a wall of resistance to the concept of gradual withdrawal." At the urging of a colleague, Dr. Nyswander decided to write a paper on the subject and, in January, 1950, "Withdrawal Treatment of Drug Addiction" by Marie Nyswander, M.D., appeared in the *New England Journal of Medicine*. "The purpose of this paper," she wrote, "is to present a plan of withdrawal treatment that may be utilized by the physician in general practice." She detailed the multiple difficulties involved, but explained how they could be overcome "with the resources available in the average community."

It was the first paper of its kind, Dr. Nyswander believes, in a general medical journal. "I thought that once the paper was done, I'd have nothing more to do with addicts. The paper seemed to solve the problem of how to withdraw them, and that was all I knew. But I learned that once you write a paper, you're an authority. At the time, moreover, I was one of only three psychotherapists in New York who had been at Lexington. As people became more alarmed about the increase in addiction, we were more and more sought out in crises. The other two finally backed out of the whole problem. They wouldn't handle any addicts. I didn't throw up my hands, perhaps because I'm a woman and was therefore enough of a masochist to go on."

"Anyway," Dr. Nyswander continues, "as a result of the paper and of other doctors' knowledge that I was treating addicts, I eventually became inundated with them. People would call me up and I'd assume the obligation, handling addicts in whatever stumbling way I could because there was hardly anyone else. I had started by thinking there was only one solution—go to Lexington and stay there for four months.

But now, I was seeing addicts outside a prison; and from that experience, I realized, first of all, that the stereotypes of the 'dangerous drug fiend' were wrong. They didn't steal from me. They didn't mug me. They did want help."

Dr. Nyswander also discovered that in her paper on withdrawal for the *New England Journal of Medicine*, she had been wrong in her conviction that "to ensure the success of withdrawal treatment, the physician must insist on hospitalization for all patients." Soon after the "cold turkey" incident at Bellevue, she had her first experience in supervising a home withdrawal. A doctor in New Jersey was treating an old man who had been addicted in a New York hospital following an operation. The doctor called her for advice, and she told him to send his patient to Lexington. "But he's an old man," the doctor objected. "You can't send him to prison. He'll probably die there." Accordingly, over the telephone, Dr. Nyswander dictated a schedule for withdrawal. The New Jersey physician checked with her daily, and within three weeks the old man was successfully withdrawn.

In the years since, Dr. Nyswander has withdrawn hundreds of addicts at home. "If the addict really wants to get off," she maintains, "and if there is someone in the family — or a friend — who is responsible and will follow my instructions, I can usually supervise that kind of withdrawal on the telephone. It generally takes three to four days, but can extend up to two weeks. Unfortunately, most of those who are withdrawn, with no other treatment or follow-up, sooner or later relapse."

Doctors who want to prescribe narcotic drugs to their patients must have a special license, issued by the Treasury Department, under which the Federal Bureau of Narcotics functions. During the years in which Dr. Nyswander was most actively involved in home withdrawals, she did not prescribe narcotic drugs as substitutes for heroin in the initial stages of treatment because she had never applied for such a license.

Instead, she used tranquilizers, such as Miltown and Thorazine, along with vitamins and sleeping pills. "I have a license now, because I need one to prescribe methadone," she explains. "The reason I didn't have one all those years was that I was afraid. My commanding officer at Lexington had advised me not to get a license, because once addicts knew I had one, they'd keep pressing me to give them drugs. But the real reason I didn't apply was that if a doctor prescribes narcotics for drug addicts, he runs the risk of having to defend his use of the license to the Federal Bureau of Narcotics, and I was a coward. I wasn't prepared emotionally or financially for court battles. Informers, incidentally, had been sent to my office from time to time to see if I ever referred patients to doctors who *would* give them drugs. I never did. Now that I do have a license, there's no conflict with the Federal Narcotics Bureau because our research with methadone is being done in hospitals."

The fact that, without a narcotics license, Dr. Nyswander was able to develop methods of home withdrawal, hardly satisfied her. There was still the root problem of rehabilitation. The more experience she had with addicts, the more convinced she was that much more had to be learned about the nature of addiction and the psychodynamics of the addict.

In 1955, therefore, Dr. Nyswander organized in New York a research workshop in the treatment of drug addicts as voluntary patients. It was the first such project to accept patients who were still addicted to drugs and who were voluntary outpatients. Dr. Nyswander financed the entire project herself, hiring a secretary and taking care of all incidental expenses. "Essentially," she says, "I was curious. I got together thirty of my friends and said, 'Let's see what will happen if we take the first hundred addicts who call us.'" The staff of the Narcotic Addiction Research Project, as it was formally called, consisted of seven psychiatrists, eleven psychologists, and twelve social workers. Some of the patients were referred to the project by physicians, social agencies, hospitals, and the House of Detention. Others heard of it from addicts. Dr. Nyswander was the screening psychiatrist. After an initial interview, she decided which of the therapists on the staff might be best suited to the particular patient. "She was the logical person for the assignment," says Dr. Charles Winick, one of the psychologists involved. "With her attractiveness, charm, and humor, she was able to minimize the threatening nature of the interview situation."

Fees for the treatment were decided by the patient and his therapist on the basis of ability to pay. No patient was refused treatment because he hadn't enough money. From September, 1955, to July, 1956, seventy patients made an initial telephone contact with Dr. Nyswander. Half that number went on to work with one of the therapists on the staff. At the end of a year, thirteen patients remained in treatment. Ten of them had stopped using drugs, two had decreased their habits, and one took drugs occasionally.

"Our tentative results," Dr. Nyswander and four colleagues summarized the year's experience in the *American Journal of Orthopsychiatry*, "suggest that some narcotics addicts may be treated on an outpatient basis by psychoanalytically trained psychotherapists who use procedures which do not differ significantly from those used in the treatment of other emotionally disturbed persons. It has been demonstrated that some drug addicts will voluntarily present themselves for psychotherapy and that they do not seem to present untoward hazards. They may be treated on an ambulatory basis while still addicted. Withdrawal for some patients can be accomplished on an ambulatory basis, although the lack of appropriate hospital facilities presents certain practical problems."

This experiment in the ambulatory treatment of addicts did much to build up proof that the addict could, first of all, be treated as a sick person while still in the community. Not all addicts had to be quarantined in a prison or a hospital.

"It was an important pioneering project," Dr. Nyswander notes. "Not that it changed the viewpoint of the Federal Bureau of Narcotics. From the start, we told them what we were doing, and a representative of the Bureau was at every one of our staff meetings. What concerned him was his feeling that the therapists weren't asking the right questions to make absolutely sure whether their patients were still on drugs. It was impossible to communicate to him that we didn't care. We were trying to establish a therapeutic atmosphere, a relationship, a confidence. In therapy, people tell the truth at their own rate. Whether a patient was being entirely truthful when he told us he was off drugs was not of primary importance. Other things we were learning about them and that they were learning about themselves were more important."

In 1957, Dr. Nyswander was involved in another research project on ambulatory treatment of addicts. Supported by an initial grant from the Newport Jazz Festival, a Musicians' Clinic was established in New York. Any addicted jazz musician who wanted psychiatric help was eligible to apply. Again, Dr. Nyswander functioned as the screening analyst. In the first year of the Musicians' Clinic, fifteen musicians, all addicted to heroin, made an initial contact. A control group of fifteen other addicted musicians was set up. These latter addicts, who were not getting psychiatric help, were roughly matched with those in therapy in approximate age, marital status, race, and degree of success and creativity as a jazz musician.

Of the fifteen who came in that first year, two finished their psychotherapy and eight were still in contact with their therapists at the end of the Clinic's third year of operation. In a report on the Musicians' Clinic for the *American Journal of Orthopsychiatry*, Dr. Nyswander and Dr. Charles Winick noted: "Those who stayed in psychotherapy were clearly sicker than those who dropped out, but their egos were strong enough to permit the expression of their anxiety. Although the expression of rage and hostility is always difficult for a drug addict, the musicians who stayed could express it in their therapy while its initial ventilation during the first few sessions may have frightened those who dropped out."

The ten patients who had remained in therapy had been off drugs for a mean period of thirty months at the close of the Clinic's third year. The five who had dropped out had been off drugs for an average of twenty-nine months. (All the patients, incidentally, had been withdrawn at their own request within two months after beginning psychotherapy). At the end of that third year, all members of the control group were still using drugs regularly. Commenting on comparative work performances, Nyswander and Winick observed that "all but one of the ten active patients and four of the five dropout patients have improved their standing in their profession and have obtained better jobs since their contact with the clinic; several current patients have more than doubled their income. Three of the members of the control group are faring better musically than they did when they were first contacted, and most of the rest are at roughly the same level. Two have deteriorated in their work situation."

The musicians were treated, not only for the symptoms of their addiction, but also to try to make them aware of their specific personality problems. Accordingly, a maximum flexibility of therapeutic approach was possible. The proportion— two thirds—of those who remained in extended treatment was much higher than had been reported in any of the small number of previous papers on the psychotherapy of addicts. Also illuminating were the case histories of the musicians prior to treatment. Before they decided to be withdrawn, "this group of patients," Nyswander and Winick wrote, "demonstrated ability to function while addicted and some also demonstrated that it was possible to take relatively stabilized dosages without *necessarily* increasing the amount ingested."

The experience with the jazz musicians, while useful,

had its limitations. The patients had started psychotherapy with comparatively stronger egos than are characteristic of most drug addicts. As Nyswander and Winick realized, "they all had a highly specialized profession and relatively high yet realistic levels of aspiration." Similarly, in the 1955 project, those addicts who had applied for treatment already possessed enough self-confidence to come forward and take part in the experiment. Hundreds, perhaps thousands of addicts knew of the 1955 clinic, but only seventy made an initial contact. Two years later, several hundred jazz musicians would have been eligible for the Musicians' Clinic, but only fifteen volunteered during its first twelve months. "At least," Dr. Nyswander summarizes both experiments, "we did show that some addicts could be sufficiently motivated to start psychotherapy while on drugs. Some were then able to stay in treatment and get off drugs."

OVER the past twenty years—through her experiences in various research projects, through her patients, and through storefront psychiatry in East Harlem—Dr. Nyswander has become more and more certain that it is nearly always misleading to generalize about addicts. Although *The Drug Addict as a Patient* included an introductory appraisal of the addict's personality, it went on to emphasize that "neither intelligence, social stratum, occupation, religion nor race seems to have any bearing on drug addiction." In a later paper, she added: "The psychiatric examination of addicts reveals that addicts comprise the entire span of psychiatric diagnosis, and in general the diagnostic categories are closely proportionate to those found in the nonaddict population. Addicts may be schizophrenic, obsessive-compulsive, hysteric, psychopathic or have simple character disorders. Although once addicted, the behavior of all addicts may closely resemble each other (at least in the social sense of behavior), basically the individuals may be very different indeed."

With these warnings heavily underlined, Dr. Nyswander will say that addicts, whatever their psychiatric diagnosis, are commonly withdrawn and have overwhelming feelings of inadequacy. The addict's early family situation may have contributed to that sense of inadequacy. In her book, Dr. Nyswander wrote that "the male addict on a conscious level looks down on his father as weak and ineffectual. Fathers are described as cowardly, weak, dominated by their wives and lacking in affection." But, "as therapy continues and the addict's hostility is expressed, another image of the father appears: the strong parent who provides for the family and who has survived his mother's domination. This is the strong image which the patient has felt incapable of living up to or competing with, the image he tries to handle by superficial criticism in an attempt to deny the father's strength, which in truth he feels is completely overwhelming." Consciously, an addict usually feels very close to his mother who in turn is likely to have been overprotective of her son. "A perfect way," Dr. Nyswander noted, "to foster a so-called mother fixation."

Most present-day addicts now begin their habit in their late teens or early twenties and continue until the late thirties when addiction frequently appears to taper off. Since it is known that narcotics diminish sexual activity severely, addiction in those years may well serve as a way of avoiding the challenges of an active sex life from adolescence up to middle age. Moreover, the period from adolescence to the late thirties also require, as Dr. Nyswander has pointed out, a man's "active assuming of responsibility, his mobilization of sufficient security and aggression to enable him satisfactorily to perform the functions of a mature adult." The addict, however, is unaggressive—and except for physicians, nurses, and other professionals who become addicted—he "rarely develops any skill or trade which would enable him to provide for himself, to say nothing of a potential family." In this area too, drugs may be a way of evading the stresses of a "normal" life.

By withdrawing from the daily competitiveness of the "square" world, the addict is left "with almost no means of obtaining satisfaction from any kind of constructive aggression." Further insuring his isolation are his self-destructive impulses. "His relationships with family and friends have perhaps been irreparably spoiled. He has usually proved so unreliable on any job that he cannot get adequate references if he should want to work. . . . Thus he creates a realistic situation which puts him out of the running, so to speak. His fears about himself become facts and construct a further barrier to normal rehabilitation."

Yet the addict is not immune from dreams of success. He indulges, however, in the magical thinking of the immature. "So great is his need for immediate recognition, for *being*," Dr. Nyswander wrote, "that he does not allow himself a period of *becoming*. He demands of himself success with very little effort. . . . Because of his anxiety, he lacks the capacity for long term planning toward a definite goal." Drugs "become the aggressor and do all the work. Once he has plunged the needle, the drugs give him what other men spend their lives working for: a feeling of power, a sense of security, sexual satisfaction, and so on. . . . He has succeeded in killing two birds with one stone: maintaining his passivity and withdrawnness while at the same time experiencing the feelings of satisfaction that come to the aggressor."

In her book and in subsequent articles, Dr. Nyswander has emphasized that relapse is a part of the disease of addiction because, along with the pharmacological factors involved, "the conscious mind never forgets it has a darn good solution to the problems of life and, in periods of stress, it will revert to the use of drugs."

Dr. Nyswander continues to stress that there is no way of determining who—no matter what his family situation—will become a drug addict. "There are so many nonaddicts with family backgrounds similar to those of most addicts. Why haven't they chosen drugs? Then, whatever personality structure the addict had to begin with becomes changed by the very fact of his addiction and by his being outside of society. He'll never be the same. He's had a profound experience. Call it, if you will, a profound psychopharmacological experience. That's what I meant when I said that after the shattering knowledge of failure they go through, they may come back with a clearer vision of themselves and other human beings than most of the rest of us are likely to get."

"You also have to remember," Dr. Nyswander adds, "that we all have the potential for chemical addiction. That's why they're so careful at Lexington when they use the staff for research. They're fully aware that anyone can become an addict. About fifteen years ago, in one hospital engaged in a large study on pain, the researchers were convinced they had no predisposition to addiction. Every one of them came perilously close to being addicted. They almost frightened themselves to death."

"I will grant," Dr. Nyswander says, "that the majority of the addicts mentioned in the literature and the majority of those I've seen can be said to have the problems typical of adolescence or, in many cases, of preadolescence. However they got that way, that's where they are. How, then, do we best work with them? Can you superimpose on this kind of psyche and on these kinds of anxieties a program of rehabilitation which deprives the addict of the drugs that have stabilized him? It's like saying, 'I'll treat you for stuttering, if you'll stop stuttering.' "

There is probably no psychiatrist in the country who has

tried to rehabilitate as many different kinds of addicts as has Dr. Nyswander. In her private practice, in hospitals, in East Harlem, and in the course of her research projects, her patients have ranged from a homicidal paranoid to a graduate student at the Massachusetts Institute of Technology, the machinery of whose mind she compares to a Rolls-Royce. ("What an instrument to work with!")

The paranoid, whom she saw regularly for almost two years whenever he was out of jail, was an East Harlem addict with a long record of assault on women. An autodidact, he had read widely in philosophy and religion, and claimed to have been drawn to Dr. Nyswander primarily because he felt that her mind was on a level with his own. "Once he came in," she recalls, "with the blood still on his hands from bludgeoning a woman. There we were, just us alone. On that occasion, and on others, I was scared, especially on those days when he'd just sit and stare at me until he'd mutter, 'Don't you block *me!*' But I think I hid my fear from him. Anyway he did keep coming back. I don't know what help, if any, I was to him. I still hear from him and run into him occasionally."

The paranoid was an exception in that very few of Dr. Nyswander's other addict patients have acted out their aggressions. Most of them have either never tried regular therapy or have had little success at it, but they continue to keep in touch with her. Even addicts she has not treated for a long time maintain contact. Eventually, there is a telephone call, a letter, or a visit. "It's quite different," Dr. Nyswander says, "from the usual experience with middle-class patients in my private practice. Once the analysis is over, they work you out of their system, and you're not likely to hear from them again. But with addicts, there can be seven years of silence, and then a letter. You see, these are my friends. My relationship with these guys is for life. It's deep. I'm in their lives and they're in mine. It's a great joy to have relationships like that." Dr. Nyswander's medical colleagues and several of her addict patients agree that one of the reasons for the durability of her relationship with addicts she has treated is that although she is candid, she does not give pain. "Some of those doctors," says one addict, "use candor like a weapon, but not her."

"I have been in this particular branch of medicine for many years," says Dr. Romano Antonelli, a psychiatrist with considerable experience in treating drug addicts, "and I have met many people who speak of loving mankind as if they were making a profession of it. I mean social workers, psychologists, and the like. I'm usually very skeptical of this kind of practitioner, particularly when he denies he ever gets angry at a patient. Marie is quite something else. She has an intrinsic honesty, far beyond any result of her having been in analysis. It's part of her basic personality structure. When she talks of a patient, a colleague, or a friend and says, 'I love him,' there's nothing phony in that spontaneous affection. Similarly, her empathy with anyone who is suffering is very real."

"We may be talking," Dr. Antonelli grimaces, "about a patient who has done the most objectionable things to secure drugs, so objectionable that most of us would shun him. But she focuses on the amount of suffering *he* must be going through. And it's not put on. I remember an occasion when she had just seen a woman addict who had killed a man. The woman was brought to Marie before she was arrested. When Marie told me about it, I was concerned with the poor man who had been shot. So was Marie, but at *that* moment, she had been exposed to the addict's terrible suffering. As Marie spoke of the woman, there were tears in her eyes. In another situation, however, she is just as capable of saying of an addict, 'He makes me furious.' She can express her feelings fully, and that personality trait plays a tremendous role in her professional success."

81

Other colleagues who have either studied with Dr. Nyswander or have worked with her on various research projects also credit her warmth and femininity for some of the rapport she achieves with addicts. ("By feminine, I don't mean motherly," says one psychoanalyst. "She hardly looks like a mother.") They add, however, that along with her strength of feeling, a sharp, investigative intelligence is continually at work. "As informal as she was with her addict patients in East Harlem," Dr. Antonelli has pointed out, "she was always alert not to produce the kind of relationship that couldn't be used therapeutically later on. She knows the inner dynamics of the addict's personality better than anyone I've ever met. Very quickly she can sense at what point he is. She knows theoretically what questions to ask to open him up, and she knows what questions not to ask at a particular time."

Dr. Nyswander, for example, has many ways of making an addict feel she's genuinely interested in him without feeding his self-pity. During a snowy day a few winters ago, a patient shuffled into the East Harlem Protestant Parish Narcotics Office. He wore an overcoat he had been given. It was much too long and made him look like a condensed derelict. "He's probably getting kicks out of looking so miserable," said an addict on the street, looking scornfully through the window.

Inside, Dr. Nyswander looked at her patient, did a double take, and said, "What are you doing with a coat like that? Why don't you have it fixed? You look terrible." Two days later, the addict returned, and his coat no longer flapped about his legs. "You see," said a staff member of the Parish, "she didn't go into an elaborate psychoanalytical explanation of his need for pity or the theatrical way he was showing how miserable he felt. She spoke to him as a friend would, a friend who cared how he looked."

A former patient of Dr. Nyswander credits her straightforwardness and lack of sentimentality for having helped him acquire insight into his particular behavior patterns. Now off drugs and successfully completing an undergraduate degree in psychology, the ex-addict explains, "There's no question that she wants to help you. She's not aloof, but she also makes you understand that if you reject her help, she's not going to crack up. She's not your mother."

This young man began treatment in a state of massive self-pity, as do many addicts. After a few visits, he was startled and annoyed to find that every time he indulged in gratuitous woe, Dr. Nyswander would croon, "Oh, poor me." "Eventually," he recalls, "I'd find myself joining in. There would be the two of us, harmonizing on 'Oh, poor me.' After awhile, she stopped saying it along with me, and I'd be moaning it alone. Finally, I got bugged hearing it and I didn't say it any more. And then it occurred to me I didn't feel it any more, either."

"During the early stages of the methadone project," Dr. Nyswander said in the spring of 1967, "I gave up all my private patients, both addicts and nonaddicts. I wanted to devote all my time to the program. But in the past, I knew it was essential, in treating addicts, that I not take on the role of the suffering, self-pitying mother who hasn't smiled in ten years. When I'd first interview an addict, I'd put myself in his place and ask myself, 'Is she preaching at me?' I gave an addict no reason to feel guilt. I never let a patient say, 'I'll get off for you, Doc.' I didn't want him to get off for me. He wasn't hurting *me*. He wasn't going to make my life better if he got off drugs. What I wanted the patient to realize was that nothing would work unless he were doing it for himself, because ultimately he is responsible for what he does. What's gruesome to see is when an addict picks up an authoritative morality from the culture and tries to make it work without really feeling it inside."

"There were times," Dr. Nyswander continues, "when I

didn't take an addict as a private patient if I felt that my being a woman triggered great need on his part to go into the kind of suffering relationship he'd had with his mother. In those cases, I'd arrange for the patient to go to a male therapist. The addicts I did take into private practice were, for the most part, those who had attained a sufficient degree of masculinity, who had overcome enough of their martyrdom to their mothers so that we could work together. I didn't have that particular problem with women addicts, of course, but they were difficult to treat, at least before methadone. When women remove themselves from the conventions of society, they seem to have a harder time than men to pull themselves back up. They often go down very, very low. Also, a woman addict doesn't have to scuffle quite as much as a man to get money for drugs. She has a fairly easy source of money through prostitution and as a result, she may be less urgently motivated to get off drugs than a man who has a desperate daily problem of figuring out how to score. I had as good a relationship with my women patients as I did with the men, but I did not have as good results."

Although adolescents are particularly resistant to treatment, Dr. Nyswander has through the years established contact with a considerable number of fifteen- and sixteen-year-olds. "We talk about music or whatever area their joyousness—or their search for it—is pulling them toward. The idea is to find some experience of mutual pleasure. After all, when I was an adolescent, I searched in every possible direction for pleasure; and later, when I was an intern, I did the lindy hop from the Village to Harlem. I have some idea of what they're looking for. Often they would stay only a short time after they first came, but they'd return in five or six years. I consider that doing well on their part.

"I'm still in touch with one who's in his early thirties. When I first saw him, he was the leader of a teen-age gang that prided itself on using brains instead of guns. We'd roar at the devices we'd think up to outwit the gang on the next block. His ideas were usually better than mine. He stayed in therapy for two years—while he was still on drugs. He kicked by himself later on, went back to school, and is now married and has a child. He occasionally helps out addicts who stumble across his way."

When she is in private practice—and now that the methadone program has passed its first stage and is being expanded, she intends to return to private practice—a determinant for whether Dr. Nyswander agrees to take a patient, addict or nonaddict, is her ability "to hear a voice in him. Some spark that gives me a clue as to whether we can establish a relationship. Humor is one of the things I use in the initial interview to see how we get along. If they misinterpret my humor, it's likely they ought to be seeing someone else."

Humor, often wry, is pervasive in Marie Nyswander's life style. So is an uncommon zest for experience. She loves jaunty cars—a favorite for a long time was a fire-engine-red Austin-Healey—and she delights in zooming along country roads. She takes great pleasure in listening to chamber music and German lieder. Her musical tastes also extend to jazz, rock 'n' roll, and folk rock. In jazz her bent is toward the relatively modern—Miles Davis, Charlie Parker, Nina Simone. "I don't like Dixieland," she says, "It brings out the military in me." When traveling between hospitals, she almost invariably turns on her car radio to rock 'n' roll stations. "I dig the Beatles, the Mamas and the Papas, and many of the new groups. The beat is so alive and their lyrics are really saying something about being open and being in contact with what's real."

Dr. Nyswander's most passionate avocation is Greece. Some eight years ago she made her first trip there. "I didn't care one way or the other when I started," she recalls, "but when I arrived, as I was riding up a street in Athens, I started to cry. I felt I was home. As usually happens with me,

I had to see and feel Greece before realizing what it meant to me. Hearing or reading about it were not enough."

Having emotionally identified with Greece, Dr. Nyswander characteristically proceeded to an intellectual absorption in Greek literature and history. She learned the language, which she can now read and speak moderately well, and she began to collect Greek art, particularly amphorae. "I guess you could say," Dr. Nyswander said a couple of years ago, "I found my soul in Greece. But I have found something of the same freedom in talking to drug addicts. It took me a while to connect the two experiences. The Greeks represented reality and truth. The great Golden Age was joyous. The maenads, the dryads, all of those minor divinities inhabited every brook. There were gods in trees, Zeus on Mount Olympus, and Poseidon in the ocean. It was impossible to live there without having a joyous reaction to a stream, to everything around you. And so idealism could flourish. There was room for it."

"But," Dr. Nyswander stopped and lit a cigarette, "the truth and honesty which were so pervasively evident then can be found only between the lines in society today. Yet I have found some of this openness to direct experience among addicts. Addicts are forever pursuing experience. Oh, they have problems accepting what they feel and want, but some of them have such enormous potential for growth and joy and for an honest role in society."

IT HAS become Dr. Nyswander's conviction that many addicts will be able to activate their potential for growth, joy, and an honest role in society as a result of methadone. She cites as one of many examples a thirty-six-year-old Puerto Rican named Louis who had been one of her storefront patients in East Harlem. "He had never really worked in his life," Dr. Nyswander says. "I got him into the project when I met him on the street one day. For a week before he'd been sleeping on rooftops and in the subway. Since he's been on methadone, all craving for heroin has gone. He's gotten his high-school-equivalency diploma and he works seven days a week at Manhattan General Hospital. So do many of the others on the project. You can't slow them down.

"Once Louis, for instance, had convinced himself that methadone worked for him, such an excitement seized him! He had happiness by the horns and he wouldn't let go. And he *looks* so good! Louis has recovered his thirst for life. And, like the others on the project, he hasn't lost that extra dimension of perception that came out of his having been at the very bottom. The humor of Louis and the others is still delicious, and they are not judgmental. The only way they do make a judgment on others in the program is if one of them tells a lie; but even then they try very hard to understand why the lie had to be told."

"For much of my life, the main thing on my mind was heroin," Louis said to Dr. Nyswander after he'd been in the methadone program for several months. "When the desire for heroin calls, you've got to answer it. Just as when I get an itch, I've got to scratch." He grinned. "Now I'm not itching anymore."

By contrast, in the time before Dr. Nyswander had explored the possibilities of methadone, there was the case of a young man I shall call Carl who was compelled to answer the imperious call of drugs and thereby wasted an extraordinary potential. When I first saw him in 1963, he was twenty, very shy, and exceedingly intelligent. Dr. Nyswander at the time was practicing storefront psychiatry in East Harlem. Carl had resisted any form of treatment until he came to see her in her tenement office. He had, in fact, carried her name in his pocket for two years before finally going for an interview in 1962. For the next couple of years he traveled often to East Harlem to see her. Several times she withdrew him from drugs; always he had relapsed.

On a cold February afternoon a few years ago, Carl talked with me about his addiction. "It's a delusion," he said, "that's hard to give up. When you're on, you feel good in the face of hang-ups. You know the hang-ups are still there, but the tension and anxiety associated with them are greatly moderated. Drugs give you great *immediate* gratification. You know that as soon as you cook it up and shoot it, bing, bang, you've got what you want. You have something that *you* have set up as a goal. And it doesn't have to be worked at slowly, bit by bit. You can do it within a matter of minutes after you've decided to. Or, at worst, in a matter of hours if you have to take that long to cop some drugs. It's right there. I know drugs don't solve any of my problems. But they dissolve them. Temporarily. Supposing I had a—let's say—constructive goal. I'd have to work toward it slowly, day by day, year by year, with little or no gratification. I'm afraid to face that, but with drugs, they become the goal itself. They become life itself."

Yet, as is the case with most addicts, Carl admitted he was disturbedly ambivalent about his addiction. He was under constant pressure from his family to withdraw. He was persistently confronted with the uncertainty involved in going to harried and sometimes dangerously irresponsible men to buy his needs. Between shots, Carl, therefore, was usually depressed.

"I don't know what's going to happen to me," he said as he rose to go next door to see Dr. Nyswander. "My plans vary from minute to minute. Most probably I'll wind up in a mental hospital, because I'm pretty out of it. I'm pretty sick. Or maybe it'll be suicide, although I don't have the strength for that now. Or else jail. Why do I keep coming back to her if I'm that dragged? Because she's a very beautiful woman. I mean she moves, thinks, feels very harmoniously in terms of everything that's opposed to death. It's instinctive with her. She just can't do anything else." Carl hesitated, as if wanting to say more. He spread his hands in a gesture of hopelessness. "I can't make words do any more than that."

Two weeks after that conversation, I went to see Dr. Nyswander and found her obviously anxious. She held up a sweater. "Ever seen a stab wound before?" There was a rip down the right side of the sweater, and dried blood. "Carl's," she explained. "He was standing on a street corner in East Harlem. An addict he didn't know asked him if he had any drugs on him. Carl said he hadn't, and the man suddenly pulled a knife, chased him into the middle of the street, and stabbed him. He came in an hour ago with blood all over him." She pursed her lips. "And there are so many analysts who still won't take *this* kind of patient. What are you supposed to say? 'I can't take you, Carl, with all that blood.'

"This was more than an accident. Every addict has to use judgment in getting drugs. And Carl is intelligent, very intelligent. Yet he was beaten up twice in the last week. Both times he went into an alley with a stranger. Part of this has to do with me and with his having carried my name around for so long before seeing me. As you open the door a little for them, you're enabling them to make more of a choice about what they want to do for themselves. Faced with this, they take one step forward and two steps back. As they're presented with some possibility of gratification—without drugs—they can't go through the door. Carl, for example, presents himself to me beaten up and now stabbed. Their masochism rises, and they feel, 'I can't make it.'

"When an analyst is confronted with this kind of situation, he can't follow the usual rules. He can't say, 'If you don't keep your appointments, I can't continue seeing you.' You have to be available to them when they want you. And you have to run the risk, as you begin to get them close to the door, of bringing out the kind of transference Carl is demonstrating now. It's not pleasant, and you begin to wonder about the danger, but it's got to be gone through. On the one hand, he wants me as a therapist. On the other, his unconscious says, 'I can't have her. I'm beaten.'

"He becomes stimulated by the deprivation of me. I'm here, but he can't let himself have me. That's why, if you reject an addict, you give him his kicks. He's asking for it."

"If you don't reject him," Dr. Nyswander abstractedly ran her hand through her hair, "he has to act. He has to kick at himself. And that presents another danger. A therapist can open the door too quickly too soon. The therapist who goes too far will push the patient too far. If, for instance, a therapist becomes all-giving and takes the patient into his home or bails him out of jail, the addict is forced into more and more severe rejections of himself. He has more to deny himself. That's been the traditional role of many addicts with all-giving families. It may get to the point at which the patient may have to kill himself to achieve that complete a rejection of what's being offered him.

"I've worked this far with many addict patients, and what's happening to Carl now is a fairly common pattern. But that doesn't make it any easier to watch. Carl has always had to pull out, to deprive himself. When he was graduated from high school with more honors than anyone at that school had ever received, he tried to commit suicide on graduation night. When he went to Harvard, he did so well he had to leave. Then he worked as a bus boy; but in two months, he was head of all the bus boys and waiters, and he had to quit *that* job. It's sad. It's so sad. Carl's genius doesn't help him. But Jesus," she snatched a cigarette from a pack on the table, "people like Carl can become so much more independent than most of those who would put Carl down now because he's an addict. He has that chance, but I don't know what will happen to him next. I bandaged him up and sent him home."

A few days later, on a Saturday afternoon, Carl called Dr. Nyswander and asked to see her. He spent most of the day and the next day as well talking with her. As a present, he had brought Dr. Nyswander a dozen of his favorite classical albums. Besides the records, Carl left a manuscript, detailing his experiences as an addict during the preceding four years.

After Carl had gone home Sunday night, Dr. Nyswander said to me, "Did you know he can't listen to his records when he's off drugs? The experience is too overwhelming for him. He can allow himself to read. You can tell how much and how intensely he's read. And he's filled with the sensitivities of a writer. But the stimuli from all his involvements with life on every level become too much for him, and he throws up in despair. In some way, he has come to feel that the prospect of ecstacy in exploring the unknown must be bad. After all, there's so little of it in the society around him. And if it's bad, he has to pull away from it, hide from it. All that joy in experiencing his books and records can't get out." She was silent for a moment. "But he was in good spirits when he left. Maybe he's beginning to find some order in his misery."

On Monday night, Carl took an overdose of barbiturates at home, and went into a coma. Dr. Nyswander had rushed to see him and had consulted with Carl's brother, a physician. The next morning, she was waiting in her office to hear from Carl's family about his condition. He had not yet been moved to a hospital. By noon, she started calling his home, but there was no answer. Nor could she reach Carl's brother.

At 1:00 P.M., it was time for her to start for Metropolitan Hospital where she was on staff at the time. She would then proceed to her tenement office in East Harlem. Dr. Nyswander threw on a coat, stepped into the hallway, and pressed the elevator button. "I hope," she said grimly, "that you're not seeing another life lost in the cause of the Federal Bureau of Narcotics. I lose five to twenty addicts a year from overdoses. Last June, I lost a lovely, intelligent boy. A college boy." She banged her fist against the wall. "There's no reason! There's no reason!"

In the elevator, she leaned against the back of the car. "Over a period of years," she said, "there may be as much as a 20 percent mortality rate in any given group of addicts. You can't tell for sure because meaningful statistics in any part of this field are hard to come by. But you ask a group of addicts in East Harlem, 'How many are with you?' You'll almost always find some have died in the last few years. How can people accept these needless deaths?"

As she walked out to the street, she shook her head from side to side. "Should have done, should have done, should have done," she mumbled. "And I, I'm always faced with my own lack of courage. I knew he had been taking Dolophines for the past couple of weeks. Some doctor had given them to him. I knew he was running out that weekend. Why didn't I go out and get some Dolophine for him? But I couldn't because I don't have a narcotics license. Once again I was protecting my own skin. So my skin will be preserved and maybe a patient is going to be lost. Try living with that for awhile?" She hailed a cab. "Damn, where did I fail?"

While on her way to Metropolitan Hospital, Dr. Nyswander was explaining the nature of the program there for addicts. I mention it here in the context of what has since been discovered about methadone because the existence of methadone treatment at the time might have made an important difference in the success of the hospital's program for addicts. Methadone also, Dr. Nyswander said in 1967, might have made a crucial difference in what happened to Carl.

A narcotic addiction treatment unit had been started in 1959 as part of Metropolitan Hospital's regular psychiatric service. Located on First Avenue and Ninety-ninth Street, the hospital is in a neighborhood where addiction is endemic by contrast with the isolated and often heavily guarded institutions in which addicts are usually quarantined. There were two narcotics wards—one for detoxification and one for rehabilitation—of twenty-five beds each. Only male addicts were accepted, and each applied for admission voluntarily. The treatment center was unique in that it was used for medical teaching in conjunction with New York Medical College-Metropolitan Hospital Center. As part of their psychiatric training, medical students worked on the wards. The staff also included social workers, recreation therapists, and vocational counselors. In addition to group therapy, every patient was assigned to an individual therapist; and after the patient was discharged, he made appointments to continue seeing his therapist once or twice a week at the clinic attached to the hospital. He was also eligible to join the social club for discharged patients.

Dr. Nyswander was not involved in the actual organization of the narcotic unit at Metropolitan Hospital, but she had long advocated a voluntary treatment and research center in a community-based hospital, and she was soon on the staff. "My book," she said when the unit was started at Metropolitan, "may have helped prepare the way. If only in terms of its title. The idea was gotten across that a drug addict *can* be a patient rather than a 'fiend' or an outcast. The book helped hospital people feel easier—some of them anyway—about assuming responsibility in the treatment of addicts."

On the day of my visit with her to Metropolitan Hospital in early 1963, Dr. Nyswander walked swiftly to the elevator and went up to the fifteenth floor where the rehabilitation ward was located. To the right, as she stepped out of the elevator, a uniformed guard sat at a table at the entrance to the ward. To the left was the office of the Department of Psychiatry. Dr. Nyswander checked in at the office, greeted several of her colleagues, and strode toward the wards.

From the office door, Dr. Edward Gordon, a psychiatrist in residency at Metropolitan, watched her. Dr. Nyswander had been one of his first supervisors when he began work with addicts at the hospital. A compact, intense young man, he gestured in her direction. "Marie," he said, "probably knows more addicts in East Harlem than anyone else around here, except maybe Reverend Eddy of the East Harlem Protestant Parish. She sure can reach them. She overwhelms even *their* chronic distrust. She's not the typical, detached, 'objective' psychiatrist. And I think her patients are better off because she isn't. After all, the addict himself is very detached and needs someone to really involve him in a relationship. Otherwise he drifts away again."

Dr. Gordon began talking about his experience at Metropolitan. "I've always felt hampered in giving therapy here because we're dealing with dual objectives. We're involved with a sick patient and we're also involved with getting him off drugs. Yet these problems are not parallel. If someone is sick, you don't ask him to give up his symptoms before he's cured. And to many addicts, drugs are a tremendously important way of controlling their anxieties. The fact that we can't give them drugs while they're being treated accounts for many of our therapeutic failures. We have a tremendous rate of relapse because most of our patients aren't really ready to get off. Most come here to withdraw because of tremendous external pressures on them—from the family, from the police— not because they themselves *want* to be off drugs. And by our saying we can't treat them until they've withdrawn, we ally ourselves with that part of the world that just wants them to get off. Sure, everyone here comes in voluntarily, but ask them how many would be happy if drugs were given away free, and they'd all shout for joy."

Dr. Nyswander had returned, and was listening. "I agree," she said, "that this is still a stemming action. Here at the hospital if an addict has relapsed and he comes in groggy from too much of a dose or sick from too small a shot, you're supposed to stare deep into his eyes and say, 'No, *you* can't be rehabilitated until you're clean again. *You* can't play.' We are not dealing with those most in need of help. They're the ones who are most erratic and most likely to relapse. And those are the ones we banish because they cause management problems. So once again, we're in that whole business of trying to utilize psychiatry in a context which does not permit the full functioning of psychiatry."

"Psychiatry," she was now waving her hand vigorously, "deals with the individual and his problems. But the individual, even in a voluntary hospital setup like this one, must of necessity conform to the criteria of efficient hospital management. The result is that this is not a program for the individual, at least not for the individual who cannot conform. Now this is probably the finest hospital of its kind in the country, but even here there are limitations as to whom you can treat. It's pathetic to see some of the guys who are not 'clean' walk all the way up fifteen floors and sneak past the guard simply to enjoy, however briefly, a decent place in which they can paint, eat, or simply talk. But they cause problems. They might stagger around and they might disturb people on the elevators. So you must exile them. But if you gave them drugs and *then* tried to treat them, you could have programs going for all kinds of addicts, programs which could be creative and fulfilling for everybody."

"Exactly," Dr. Gordon nodded furiously. "Certainly addiction is a psychiatric problem, but now it's first a social problem. But is that primarily the addict's fault? Look at it this way. If mothers have to work, we open up child-care centers, thereby preventing the mothers from going on welfare and allowing them to function as well as they can. Here we have a group of people who so far can't function without drugs—not all addicts, but many of them. We should, therefore, alter their environment in such a way that they're not harmful to others in obtaining drugs.

"What we first have to do is undermine the addict subculture, and we can begin by legalizing drugs. Suppose we could give them drugs at cost or close to cost. One hundred quarter-grains of morphine would come to $1.65 or so. A half dozen would keep the average addict in balance for a day, and a dozen would take care of almost any addict, no matter how high his tolerance has become. You see how cheap the drugs would be then. If we could get the medical schools which run the big city hospitals together with the Commissioner of Health and the Department of Hospitals, we could set up clinics in the hospitals with proper controls. After all, it's no major problem to set up a system whereby we could identify each addict and make sure he gets only what he's supposed to get. With clinics, addicts wouldn't have to steal to get the money for drugs, and they wouldn't have to deal with pushers."

"The important point to realize," Dr. Gordon went on, "is that it's obviously not necessary to get all addicts off drugs before we can get the criminality out of addiction. There's also another way in which legalization of drugs under medical control would undermine the addict subculture. Addicts would be dispersed all over the city instead of congregating together, as they do now, in certain neighborhoods where they know illegal drugs are more easily obtained. Where are all the schizophrenics in New York? They're all over the city. They don't get together because they have no reason to. Similarly, drug addicts are not naturally drawn to each other. They meet to find drugs. They often don't like and don't trust each other and have little in common besides drugs. Sure, they hang around street corners together— waiting—but they don't do much else together."

"Furthermore," Dr. Gordon continued, "by learning more about how each patient reacts to therapy while he's on drugs, we may be able to find out a great deal more about realistic methods of treatment. Some addicts function very well on drugs; some function badly. The latter will want to give up drugs more quickly, and the psychiatrists will then be able to concentrate on those who are left. And it's quite possible that some habits can be stabilized if drugs were available legally. I've known addicts who have managed to keep their habits fairly small and who have worked efficiently for years. There might be more of that kind of addict if the getting of drugs weren't so connected with the possibility of panic. Many addicts now are affected by fear of not being able to get enough next time. So they shoot up whatever they can get when they get it."

"Sure," Dr. Nyswander broke in. "If you were to tell me I couldn't have any cigarettes tomorrow, I'd smoke all I have today."

"Tolerances differ, of course," Dr. Gordon went on. "Various addicts would require differing amounts of drugs. Some would be able to get by with an occasional fix once or twice a week. Others may rapidly build up a large habit. In between will be the largest group, addicts who will be able to keep their habit within certain boundaries and who will also be able to keep their families together and feel themselves useful members of society."

"Another objection to the clinic idea," said Gordon, apparently convinced he had disposed of the other doubts concerning the efficacy of the idea, "is that some patients would have to come four or five times a day for shots. Well, if a long-acting capsule to medicate colds can be made, a long-acting capsule of morphine could be perfected. The addict with that kind of habit could take one such capsule in the morning and another at night."

"You're damn right," Dr. Nyswander laughed. "The drug companies would develop one very quickly indeed if they knew a million addicts would be taking it."

"And why," Dr. Gordon interrupted, "do we have to have clinics? Let's have any doctor treat them. Why should an addict's privacy be invaded by his having to show up at a clinic? Why should anyone but his doctor know he's an addict?"

"Of course," Dr. Nyswander exclaimed. "Having individual doctors treat individual patients is much more sensible. In the first place, there's no chance to develop an intimate relationship in the context of the way a clinic has to be managed. But a doctor, once oriented in addiction, could develop a treatment program suited to the particular needs of each of his patients. Doctors aren't fools, and it's hardly a complicated problem to administer drugs. Once, moreover, there's a personal relationship between the doctor and his patient, if an addict felt he wanted to reduce his habit, he could talk it over with his doctor. Or if he wanted to increase his dosage, he could talk *that* over. The point is that the patient should be able to feel he has his own doctor rather than just someone dispensing pills."

"We already know of many cases," said Dr. Nyswander, "in which a sympathetic doctor working with addicts has had patients return up to four years after the first visit with a sincere desire to undertake a cure. The important thing is for the addict to know there is someone who accepts his problem, even though he himself may not have made up his mind yet about stopping the habit completely. There are general practitioners who don't know how much they have helped addicts. I do know because over and over again I ask addicts to recall the longest period during which they've been off drugs. Maybe an addict will say two years, and I'll ask him how he accomplished it. He'll tell me that a general practitioner gave him a substitute drug for a couple of days and he took himself off and stayed off. The general physician who has taken the trouble to help the addict plays a big role. On the other hand, if a treatment setup is impersonal, addicts will turn to each other for comfort and understanding."

"Sometimes," said Gordon, "I get very discouraged at the slow progress we're making toward an intelligent approach to addiction. It seems so hopeless until the next time I see her," he turned to Dr. Nyswander. Unexpectedly, Dr. Gordon laughed. "You know, if there were more addicts in this country, we'd have a woman President." He paused. "I'd vote for her too."

Dr. Nyswander frowned. "But the question is," she pretended deep concern, "do I want to be President?"

"As an incentive," Dr. Gordon volunteered, "you can

have 150,000 acres of poppies—with a farm subsidy."

"Man," said Dr. Nyswander, "what have you been taking today? You're swinging."

As Dr. Nyswander and Dr. Gordon moved off to a corner of the Department of Psychiatry office to discuss a case, a young jazz musician came out into the corridor from the rehabilitation ward. He had already been detoxified at Metropolitan Hospital six times and was now determined to stay off drugs, he explained, because he had an offer to join one of the most prestigious of the jazz combos if he kicked his habit. The musician heard Dr. Nyswander's laughter from inside the office, and said, "I really dig her. I don't see her but once in awhile, but each time she does something for me. She makes you answer for yourself. She brings it down front for you to decide for yourself. Man, I think she should take over the whole problem for the whole country. She should be the President's man in charge of narcotics."

Dr. Gordon had returned and smiled at finding himself in agreement with the patient about Dr. Nyswander's qualifications for the post of federal czar of narcotics.

The musician was getting nervous and started shifting from foot to foot. "Man, I get so bored here. Well, later, got to get back."

"Look at him," Dr. Gordon said as the musician passed the uniformed guard. "Suppose he could never withdraw. Suppose he got his drugs legally and regularly. What possible harm could that guy do? He's not destructive. In fact, it's the unusual addict who has had any kind of real criminal record before addiction. Consider how young most addicts are when they become addicted. They're hardly hardened criminals in their teens. Oh, some of them may have lifted something out of the five and dime or stolen a car when they were kids; but that's the kind of adolescent 'crime' you find in Westchester as well as in East Harlem. It's only when they have to start scuffling for drugs that they turn to stealing or prostitution."

Dr. Gordon put on his coat and walked toward the elevator. He was joined by Dr. Nyswander. "I suppose we're making progress in a way," Dr. Gordon said with small conviction. "Slowly the attitude is getting across that addicts should be treated as medical problems. Some federal officials and more of even the local cops have stopped saying that they all ought to be put in jail."

"Now," Dr. Gordon noted sardonically, "the trend is toward building big new hospitals for them. We don't need that many more hospital beds. This is not advanced tuberculosis. These people can function without spreading disease. They're a danger to society only because of what they do to get drugs. You can remove the addicts' danger to society without building a lot of hospitals. No, what we need is courage in official circles so that the addict is allowed to obtain his drugs legally until he has sufficient motivation and strength to get off by himself, if he ever gets that far. But I don't see any courage among the politicians. Building hospitals in this context is hardly an act of courage."

"It's pretty futile the way we're going now, even here," Dr. Gordon looked around him as he went through the front door of the hospital. "They say, 'It's all we can do.' It's *not* all we can do. It's all we can safely do without too much trouble and without having to anticipate too much trouble."

Later that afternoon, Dr. Nyswander, in her office on 103 Street, was still trying to get information about Carl. Neither his parents nor his brother had called. "Families of addicts are often strange," she shook her head ruefully. "In some ways, and this isn't judging them, they act like drug addicts. When a son is in trouble, the parents are terribly anxious to get your help at that moment. They'll promise anything. But when the pressure is off, they don't let you know what's happened. They leave you. You have to ask yourself, 'Did he get off drugs or didn't he?' Or, in this case, 'Is he alive or isn't he?' It's a little hard to take when a death is imminent."

No patient had yet come, and she began to discuss Dr. Gordon's theory that legalization of drugs might help some addicts stabilize their habits. "It's possible. People's anxieties are different and they put different drains on drugs on different days and at different times of life. Now Carl, I would expect, is the kind of addict who probably could be maintained on a fairly regular dosage. I've also known addicts who were schizophrenics or were in a schizophrenic-like process, and I tend to think that if drugs were legalized, many of them would be able to control their habits. I'm not implying, mind you, that drugs help a schizophrenic. I don't *know*." The last word was an exclamatory burst of exasperation. "Here is a whole area of basic research in that disease through which we might be able to find out a great deal about schizophrenia. But they won't let us."

ON THAT day in 1963, I left Dr. Nyswander in her office when a patient came in, and went next door to the East Harlem Protestant Parish's Narcotics Committee office where a half-dozen addicts and Reverend Lynn Hageman, Director of the Committee, were seated on folding chairs in a semi-circle, drinking coffee and talking.

On the bulletin board, someone had put up a large sheet of white paper on which he had neatly written:

From a book titled The Day on Fire. *It is the story of the French poet, Rimbaud. It begins thus: "World, I salute you. I put my thumb to my nose, with the fingers well spread,*

103

and I say to you, 'Baise mon cul.' You may do as you like,
you may strike back at me, you may condemn me, mock me,
insult me, imprison me, torture me. But you will never
defeat me."
To me this is an example of a man who is not afraid of
life, and the problems of living. He is also a rebel and is
telling the world around him, "Go to hell."

To the right of the endorsement of Rimbaud was a crude
sketch of an addict giving himself a shot. Underneath it was
the caption, "When will it ever end? Never?" The "Never"
had a line through it, and a different hand had written, "When
you dig yourself."

The atmosphere in the office was convivial, and everyone
appeared relaxed except for a short, thin Puerto Rican named
José. He was speaking with mounting intensity. "I got no
choice. I need to steal. But around here, what are you going
to get? A little radio that someone paid five dollars down and
ten dollars a week? The one good suit the guy has hanging
in a closet? It's better to work in other parts of town where
the people can afford it."

The other addicts ignored the monologue. "So, like last
week," Mike, a tall, broad Negro said mockingly, "the
psychiatrist at Manhattan General said, 'I have a new
diagnosis for you.' Man, I sat on the edge of my chair, waiting
for a new psychosis. And you know what he said? He said,
'You're full of crap.' " Mike and the others guffawed.
Reverend Hageman, a stocky man in his thirties with a crew
cut and a broad, benign-appearing face, laughed the loudest.

"When I was at Riverside," said Tom, a soft-spoken white
man in his early twenties, "my diagnosis was pseudo-stupidity."
There was another round of guffaws.

"You know something," Mike proclaimed. "We're all
masochists. Every one of us who's on drugs. Each of us in our
own way goes to the crying wall. You know, I had things so

nice for so long. But I couldn't stand to see them so nice, and I had to tear them up. Now," he stretched and yawned, "I'm in a big search." Mike grinned. "I'm looking for the way-out outlet. I don't want to be just schizoid. I want to be a *complete* schizophrenic. Way out in space where nobody can do anything to me or bother me in any way."

Reverend Hageman smiled. "What you're looking for is that grand psychosis in the sky?" Everyone laughed.

"In the meantime," said Mike, "I'll take heroin. I love it. Whoever tells you they don't like it is a liar or they're crazier than I am. It's only the hassle of getting it that bugs me."

Juan, a man in his late twenties, joined the group. He had been off drugs for a month. Mike asked him how he felt. "Scared, man," said Juan. "I don't want to fall again. If I fall now, I may never get up. You know how it works," he turned to Tom. "You start back on and you feel terrible because you're letting somebody down. Each time you feel a little lower, and the more guilty you feel, the more heroin you take. Then you figure, what the hell, you can't turn back the clock."

"What clock?" said Tom. "It stops. For me, it does. Certain parts of the day are blank. Hell, around here a kid on junk can grow up and never know he's growing up. Everything passes him by and he's still in the same position. He doesn't move. He gets older, and still he hasn't moved. I could leave one of those guys out on the street, go away for five years, and when I'd come back, he'd still be in the same spot. Man, I don't want to die while I'm still alive. But it's hard, man. You lose confidence in yourself, other people say you can't make it, and you begin to believe you can *never* make it, no matter how hard you try. Soon as something goes wrong, you say, 'Yeah, they're right. I can't make it.' And you blow your chances."

"You know what it is when you lose confidence?" Juan interrupted. "You don't love yourself and you don't love nobody. I've got kids I've never been a father to, when you come down to it. I don't know if I ever loved them or not. I never did nothing for them. My boy would say, 'Let's go to the show.' I wasn't interested in no show. I was interested in a fix. I probably hurt that kid. If I look back, I must have not cared very much for him. Things like that can turn a kid around to do wrong things, especially if he idolizes you. Then it wouldn't matter how much love anybody else gave him. He'd still feel neglected. I caught him sniffing glue last week. I grabbed him and told him I never wanted to see him in the same pickle I was in. But there's nothing I can do for that kid. I can't help him unless I can do something for myself."

Tom leaned back, rubbed his face, and said, "Yeah, those kids are something else. Last night, I saw three of them— they were maybe twelve or thirteen—sniffing a bag. They offered me some. They respect me because they figure I know all about it. My brother, now, he's something else. He's fifteen and he's making it in school. He wants to go to college, so my father is skimping and kicking me in the ass every day to send him. I may do wrong, but he'll be O.K. You know what he does? He sits down and types himself letters. And he mails them. Like, 'Dear Sir, from unknown sources I have heard that you are a great baseball player. We would like to have you on our club. Signed, general manager, New York Yankees.' "

There was silence. Tom seemed to be pondering his brother's capacities for success. Mike sprawled in his chair and wagged his feet at Tom. "He's thinking this way *now*," Mike said, "but he ain't out of here yet."

"Listen," said Tom, "the principal of his school stopped and shook my brother's hand."

"Yeah," Mike answered, "but if he's like most of the kids around here, he's bound to get more and more curious about everything as he grows up. He's going to want to experience everything about life."

106

He looked meaningfully at Tom. "Everything."

A newcomer had joined the group. A Puerto Rican in his early thirties, squat and swarthy, he spoke with a singular blend of earnestness and wry resignation. "By 1970," he suddenly announced, "75 percent of the country will be hooked on drugs. This will be the cool country. Everybody will be high. You better believe it, Jim. This is going to increase so much, it won't be funny. It's the times. But once 75 percent of the country gets on," the Puerto Rican smiled bleakly, "they'll change the word. Especially once the big wheels are on, they won't call it being a junky."

"Or else," Reverend Hageman speculated, "the word will be a badge of honor. Tell me, what if we had clinics now? What if drugs were legal?"

The newcomer sat down, lit a cigarette, tilted his head, ruminated, and predicted, "Then you'll find out who the real junkies are. A lot of the fellows, especially the young ones, get on because they're not supposed to. If drugs get legalized, some of them may stop their habits. Me, myself, I'd register as soon as I could."

"Maybe," said Tom, "maybe the day is coming when I go into a hospital, and if I feel terrible, they'll give me more than an aspirin or a tranquilizer. Mike, you think that day is coming?"

Mike shook his head negatively. "I hate to say it, but I don't think so. Not in any future I can see."

Pete, a young Negro addict who had been silent until then, got to his feet. "I'm against it," he said as he began to pace the room. "Giving people the stuff is wrong. Man, this is a synthetic heaven you're giving people. You're making it so they can never be at their best. So long as you're on, you can't enjoy the things you can do when you're normal. Like a sunset or a sunny day. The weather doesn't even come into it when you're on, except when it's very cold. No, man, it's wrong. The state will be the junky's mother."

107

"Oh, man," Mike said with evident disgust. "You're look-ing for punishment and you want all of us to suffer with you. Look, there's *got* to be a better system than the one we're in. Hell, this is no system at all. Do you dig spending all your time trying to cop? Dealing with nuts? Getting burned by some pusher who gives you a five-dollar bag of salt or milk sugar or just takes your bread and doesn't come back? You dig boosting and cracking cribs and looking out for cops? You dig the panics?"

Tom smiled. "You remember the one a year and a half ago?"

"Yeah," said Juan, brightening. "That was a time. Every-body ran out. Nobody had anything. Well, some did, but the smart ones went and hid to keep from getting killed."

"Guys were lying all over 117 Street," Mike snorted. "There was a lot of cold turkey up here for three weeks."

"There were women who showed up here in the office," Tom added, "women I never knew were on. Housewives, you know."

"I saw one guy," Mike remembered in wonderment, "with a big roll of bills. He took a hundred dollar bill and waved it around out on the corner on 100 Street. He said he'd give it for one shot. Nobody moved. And then the cat tore up the bill."

"There was this girl," Juan broke in. "She had some stuff and she began to deal in a hallway. Man, it looked like fifty guys came in with her. She got panicky and said she wouldn't sell any more. One guy pulled a knife and stuck it in her head, and they all fought for the stuff."

"I saw a guy get caught dealing dummies in a vestibule," Mike said. "This other cat took a taste from the bag, and he began yelling, 'You sold me a dummy!' He took out a gun, the rest of us hit the wall like postage stamps, and he blew the dealer away." Mike scratched his chin, and looked at Pete. "You dig all that, huh?"

"What I'm saying," said Pete, "is you don't make sick people better by keeping them sick."

"Well, baby," Mike answered, "you don't have to worry. Legalization won't happen here for a *long* time. You know, too many people here would lose a lot of bread if the junk was free. Everything here is money, money, and more money. Not that you guys are any better."

Mike pointed at Pete. "Suppose you come to me all strung out. You're sick. So I'm not going to turn you down. All right. So I take a fall and I come out of jail greasy as a pork chop. I come to you and the only reason you help me out is because I did it for you. But suppose another time, I had cut you off. Then it's later for me, right? You don't think about the time I gave you a fix. You remember the time I turned you down. That's the way all of you are. That's what I am, man. I don't trust nobody anymore. You're in a dog-eat-dog world. You got to look out for number one. When you can't do that, you can't do nothing. You got to wake up to that."

Mike walked to the door, walked back again, and scowled at no one in particular. "Almost thirty years," he snapped, "and what do I have to show for it?"

"You're still here," Tom said softly.

"Why the chip today, Mike?" Reverend Hageman asked.

"That ain't no chip. I got a log, a boulder on my shoulder." Mike laughed. "I got to cut it down to fit me. It ain't fitting me now."

A tall, thin, disheveled Negro rushed into the office. He ran to Reverend Hageman. "I can't find him," he said, his voice cracked. "I can't find him anywhere. That cop who's always on me. Damn it, today when you say you'll talk to him, he's nowhere."

"It's all right," said Hageman. "He's bound to be around tomorrow."

It was a little past five and Dr. Nyswander, her office hours over, came into the office. She looked tired, accepted a cup of coffee from Tom, and sagged into a chair. In a few minutes, she was revivified, smiled a farewell to the addicts and the staff, and strode out into the street. She walked into a restaurant on Second Avenue, made a telephone call, and frowned as she came out of the booth. Carl was no longer in a coma, but it was not yet possible to determine whether he had suffered any permanent brain damage from the overdose of barbiturates.

IN THE months after Carl took the overdose of barbiturates, Dr. Nyswander brooded about ways of finding out
more about what forms of treatment might be effective with
an addict while he was still on drugs. For a time, she thought
of financing a research project of her own and prepared to do
battle with the Federal Bureau of Narcotics; but then, in
October of 1963, a series of events began that made a private
project unnecessary.

Dr. Vincent P. Dole, a research physician and professor
at the Rockefeller Institute, had finished a year's exhaustive
study of addiction, which included reading Dr. Nyswander's
book, and he asked to see her. The two doctors had a number

111

of conversations, as a result of which he invited her to work with him on a research project at the Institute on York Avenue, overlooking the East River. This hospital, which has fifty beds, is used only for research.

To help prepare the hospital staff, including the nurses, for the new work, Dr. Nyswander brought addicts to the Institute during the month before the project was to begin. There were conversations with them, and afterward the nurses, for whom Dr. Nyswander has a deep admiration, did a good deal of reading about addiction on their own. It was then decided to admit two "hard-core criminal addicts." Elaborate security precautions were taken in an isolated wing of the hospital. Safety glass protected hospital medication, additional locks were provided, the security personnel was alerted, and an outside security agency was also hired.

In the January, 1967, issue of *The Bulletin*, a publication of the New York State District Branches of the American Psychiatric Association, Dr. Nyswander described the start of the research. "The first patient," she wrote, "was a 34-year-old single male of Italian extraction, and the second, a 21-year-old single male of Irish background. Both had a history of drug use for eight years, had spent several years in prison for possession of drugs and theft, and had made numerous attempts to get off drugs by detoxification in voluntary hospitals and in the federal hospital in Lexington. One patient had gone to California in his desperation to remain drug-free. Both patients had tried psychotherapy. Both had dropped out of high school in the first year. The I.Q.'s of the patients, as measured on the Wechsler-Bellevue Intelligence Scale, were 120 and 124."

These first two addicts came in, Dr. Nyswander later explained to me, "because they knew they'd get drugs and because they wanted to get off the street for awhile. We were given a free hand by the Institute, and I had the watchful, perceptive, analytical guidance of Dr. Dole. The best thing that ever happened in this field was his getting into it; the success of this project rests squarely on him, in my opinion. There were no problems with the Narcotics Bureau because we were working in a hospital. Dr. Dole told me, 'Marie, nobody's holding you back now. You can do anything you want to do.' And I suddenly realized that I wasn't at all sure that I *knew* what I wanted to do. I'd heard the term 'legalized drugs' all these years, and used it myself, too, but now I had to ask: What did it really mean? What medical procedure?

"Well, we started the addicts on morphine, a quarter of a grain four times a day. In three weeks, in order to keep them comfortable, we had to go up to eight shots a day of an increased dosage, a total of ten grains a day. Obviously, it was going to be impractical to devise a maintenance program on morphine. Also, on morphine the patients were rendered practically immobile. Much of the time they sat passively, in bathrobes, in front of a television set. They didn't respond to any of the other activities offered them. They just sat there, waiting for the next shot. One thing I did find out was that there were no problems with the patients. They cooperated beautifully and honestly. They had no desire to go out and cop heroin, because they didn't have to. They didn't need any sense of adventure in connection with their addiction.

"But," she continued, "there they sat, their interests ebbing and flowing in rhythm with the morphine injections. I was confronted with an abysmal lack of knowledge of what to do next. And then there was an accidental circumstance. We switched them to methadone, a drug that had been synthesized during the Second World War by German chemists looking for inexpensive morphine substitutes. At the end of the war, the American government seized the formula, along with thousands of others, to be turned over to American drug manufacturers as an 'open patent.' We knew that it was a very effective pain-killer, that it had long-acting properties and minimal withdrawal symptoms. We also knew that it

113

could be substituted for any other kind of narcotic.

"The accident was this. We wanted to reduce the huge daily doses of morphine without subjecting the two patients to severe withdrawal symptoms. Methadone was a way to do that, but because they had been on such high dosages of morphine, we had to put them on equivalently high dosages of methadone, more than twice as large as is usually given when methadone is used to withdraw people from heroin. And to keep them comfortable during the next few days, we gave them bigger and bigger amounts of methadone. What we then discovered would probably not have been apparent if those dosages of methadone had been a lot less, as they have been in some other, not so successful experiments with methadone. From that point, my life changed, and the addicts' lives changed.

"I was still staggering back from my failure with morphine, and it was Dr. Dole who realized what was happening in front of us. Striking alterations in behavior and appearance were taking place in the two patients. The older addict began to paint industriously and his paintings were good. The younger started urging us to let him get his high-school-equivalency diploma. We sent them both off to school, outside the hospital grounds, and they continued to live at the hospital. Neither of them—although both of them had every opportunity—copped heroin on the outside. From two sluga-beds they turned into dynamos of activity. We gave them all kinds of tests while they were on methadone. We found out that methadone blocked out all other narcotics. They couldn't *feel* the effect of another narcotic while they were on methadone. Accordingly, there was no craving for heroin. We found out that methadone could be given only once a day, and that sometimes the patients were so busy they actually forgot to take it. So, in addition to freeing a patient from the need to think about drugs for twenty-four hours a day, it appears that methadone gives him another eight-hour leeway. And whatever withdrawal symptoms occur during that leeway are very mild. We confirmed the fact that the drug could be taken orally and we first put it in orange juice. As for tolerance, there was no escalation problem. The dosage remained stable. In addition, we did endless medical studies— G.I. tests, bone marrow tests, blood studies, X-rays, motor-coordination tests, psychological tests. Methadone had no deleterious effects anywhere.

"And the behavioral changes continued to take place at a dazzling rate. One addict who later went on the program told a meeting of psychiatrists, 'When you've got the craving, when you have to keep scuffling for drugs, you can never complete anything. And so you never know what you can do.' That's why all addicts tend to behave alike while they're stealing and lying and figuring out ways to cop. But when they're released from the craving and the scuffling, they begin to find out who they are, and so do we. It's tremendously moving to watch them change.

"One example of the change in addicts' behavior that has held up through the entire first three years of research has had to do with their staying in the hospital during the initial stage of the methadone treatment. Addicts have been notorious hospital dropouts, rarely staying long enough to finish most treatment plans. And often hospitals have dismissed them because of their antisocial behavior. Many of our patients had had such discharges, and few had finished earlier attempts at treatment, whatever they were. But under methadone, all our patients have remained in the hospital the full six weeks except for a few working men or women whose children were being cared for by relatives. In those cases we did give them an earlier discharge.

"As for our first two patients, both completed the requirements for their high-school-equivalency diplomas, but the younger one also wanted an unqualified high school diploma. In eighteen months he worked through three years of the high school curriculum, including mathematics, physics, English, history, and Spanish, with A grades. He went on to an engineering college on a full scholarship. The older patient completed a two-year course at horticulture school and is working in a greenhouse. They continue to take methadone and come to the hospital for weekly supplies."

After the first two patients, five more were added. "All five, once the craving and scuffling stopped," Dr. Nyswander emphasizes, "revealed quite different personalities and quite different goals, and the ability to fulfill those goals. Meanwhile, after a year, security rules at the hospital were relaxed. During the day the patients went out to school or work, and on weekends they went home, taking methadone with them."

It became clear the project was ready to be enlarged. In March, 1965, with a grant from the City of New York, Drs. Dole and Nyswander took charge of four rooms on an open medical ward of the Manhattan General Division (now the Morris J. Bernstein Institute) of the Beth Israel Medical Center. "We hired our own staff," Dr. Nyswander recalls, "and we started with six patients from different neighborhoods and different ethnic groups. We knew it wasn't feasible to go on keeping patients in a hospital for over a year, as we had been doing at Rockefeller Institute, so the first six patients stayed six weeks, free to come and go depending on their individual outside obligations. Then they returned home, and came back only once a day to get their methadone. Later, as we gained more experience with more addicts, we permitted patients, after they'd been on the program two months, to take home methadone for the weekend. If that went well, they would take home enough for two or three days at a time during the week. And, finally, some patients took home a week's supply, coming back to an outpatient department only once a week for a urine test and to take one day's supply of methadone with a nurse present.

"Another experiment we made was to take two addicts

who were working and switch them to methadone on the street. That is, they slept in the hospital for three weeks but didn't miss a day's work. With them, and with nearly all the others we've had in the project, the changes in behavior continued to be dramatic. In a week after they started, the obsessive conversations about drugs that are endemic to most addicts came to an end. And physically they looked as if they'd recovered from pneumonia. Another outstanding behavioral change was their considerateness. Addicts usually appear so self-centered and, you know, I rarely received presents from addicts in the past. Now the presents began flying back and forth, from the patients to the staff and back again. And nobody could have more cooperative patients.

"What it comes down to, Dr. Dole says, is that we take care of the pharmacological problems, leaving the addict, and everyone else, free to turn his attention to other problems. It does not strike me as relevant whether these patients ever get off methadone. Some may want to, and that's fine. What *is* relevant is that a treatment can be developed so that the addict can become a socially useful citizen, happy in himself and in society. That's much more important than whether he's on or off a medication. Admittedly, we have more to learn about methadone and a great deal more to learn about the processes of addiction. But some things we do know by now. Many research people have been coming through to examine the program, and several from Lexington thought that maybe I was the variable. Maybe my enthusiasm was carrying these people along. Of course, I had been enthusiastic for more than fifteen years and had never had results like these, but anyway, for a month in the spring of 1965 I was in Greece, and the program continued to function very well under another doctor.

"But no solution covers all problems. So far we've been taking only confirmed addicts—those addicted to heroin for five years or more. And we've admitted only those between twenty and forty. We'll have to find out how very young addicts respond to methadone. And what of those addicts who turn out to be resistant to methadone? We'll have to find out whether their unwillingness to give up the 'high' of heroin is psychological, has to do with intolerance to methadone, or has some other cause. But even with all the remaining questions unanswered, I'm convinced that we have reached a stage at which the treatment of drug addiction can become firmly entrenched in the medical profession, because there now *is* a medical procedure, a procedure that can be taught, that can be duplicated, that can be executed.

"Further research will perhaps turn up better drugs, drugs that will even be longer-acting. And there will be further work on ways to help rehabilitation. For example, some of our patients need legal advice for trouble they got into while they were still on heroin. And past police records will have to be reevaluated so that civil service and other jobs can be made available to patients on methadone according to their abilities. As I've pointed out, many of the addicts in the project are already working in hospitals. I walk in, and I see our patients working as research assistants, as secretaries, as operators of IBM machines. These are people who in the past would have been allowed in a hospital only under lock and key. Now none of the visiting research people, including agents of the Federal Narcotics Bureau, can tell which members of our staff are patients."

"Also for the future," Dr. Nyswander continues, "there will be continuing research on addiction itself: where drugs act in the body, how they are metabolized, whether narcotics are stored in the memory of the cells, the effects of narcotics on the hormonal system of the body. Now that the patient can be relieved of the craving and the lying and the stealing, these questions can be explored. And, attracted by Dr. Dole's work in the methadone project, endocrinologists, biochemists, and other scientists throughout the world are now becoming much more interested in this phase of narcotics research.

"There is yet a further dimension to be explored. We may get leads into a deeper understanding of mental illness. The behavioral changes with methadone are every bit as dramatic as the psychological phenomenon that occurs under LSD. Now, once you have a drug—LSD or a narcotic—that you can put into a patient and have resultant behavioral changes to observe and study, you've made a considerable start toward setting up procedures for future research in the field of mental health.

"And if we've done nothing else, we've proved that a patient on methadone does not seek heroin, so that it *is* possible to make a big dent in the illicit-drug traffic. Incidentally, the daily cost per patient on methadone maintenance gets progressively lower. Not only doesn't he have to steal to satisfy his craving for heroin, but simply in terms of medical costs, as the patient succeeds socially, he requires less and less of the staff's time. The cost of the methadone blockade treatment, including data collection, social services, and counseling, is approximately $2,000 per addict for the first year and $1,000 a year thereafter. Conservatively, the cost is less than one-fifth of that required to confine an addict in a hospital. And the effectiveness of the program is so much greater than any other so far."

In *The Bulletin* of the New York District Branches of the American Psychiatric Association, Dr. Nyswander has described the nature of the staff in the methadone project, and its function. "The staff consists of a physician (a psychiatrist or internist), who serves as unit director; research assistants, who are stable patients adept at handling other patients' anxieties and problems; counselors, and nurses. We divide the treatment into three phases. Phase 1 consists of hospitalization for six weeks. During this time the patient is stabilized on methadone and given a thorough medical and dental examination. Phase 2 begins with the discharge of the patient to an outpatient department and lasts for at least one year.

119

Phase 3 begins after at least one year in the community and is characterized by the patient's maintaining a responsible attitude toward his medication and living a socially useful life."

As for Phase 1, Drs. Nyswander and Dole point out in the August 1, 1966, *New York State Journal of Medicine* that "older patients, serving as research assistants, are of central importance in the initial stages of treatment. They perceive the anxieties of new patients and can speak to them with the authority of personal experience. The example of their own success inspires hope in the patients who knew them as addicts on the street only a few months before. What has been striking . . . is the rapidity with which addicts have been transformed from problem patients to dedicated staff members, some of them as soon as six months after beginning treatment. A possible explanation is that patients blockaded with methadone, and therefore indifferent to heroin, can work with drug-using addicts without feeling a threat to their own rehabilitation. The abstinent ex-addict, not protected by a narcotic blockade, remains vulnerable to readdiction and thus needs unusual strength and self-assurance to tolerate exposure to heroin."

As for Phase 2, "After discharge to the outpatient clinic, the patient lives in a rented room or at home and, if necessary, receives financial support from welfare. For most patients this is a period of major transition. Cut off from the addict world, often with no nonaddicted friends except the other patients on the treatment program, and lacking job skills, the newly discharged patient needs support and encouragement. He gets this from an identification with the program, the help of the older patients, and a friendly and perceptive attitude on the part of the staff. There is, however, no formal psychotherapy or group sessions."

Commenting further on this phase, Dr. Nyswander has noted: "The first three to six months after discharge from the hospital are the most difficult time for the patient and the most active for the staff. Each patient has a special problem or adjustment. It is easiest for those who have family or are married, either to a nonaddict wife or a wife who is also on our program. These patients do not face the loneliness that is such a burden to the isolated patient.

"The daytime might be pleasant enough, but the nights can be grueling. Some patients report going to sleep at five o'clock in the evening or sitting in their rooms watching people walk in the streets, night after night after night. We have made little attempt to cope with this problem, and many patients, during this period, drink too much while seeking the sociability of the local bar. Some patients turn to desoxyn once or twice a week. Out of 350 patients, six previous users of barbiturates have become readdicted to barbiturates and required hospitalization. But four of these patients, a year later, are working without relapse to barbiturates. The other two relapsed and were discharged from our program, which simply has not yet been geared to this particular post-charge complication."

Vital during Phases 2 and sometimes 3 are the counselors who deal with the problem of rehabilitation. "They must help the patient find a home, make welfare placements, look for a job; they must also educate him in the ways of the world, share his successes, and reduce the poignancy of his failures. . . . A majority of the patients are members of minorities, have prison records, and have obvious evidence of their past lives on their arms in the forms of 'tracks.' Our patients have had no experience in being interviewed. They have no references, skills, or education."

Accordingly, wherever it is tried, the methadone approach to addiction must be combined with effective social aid after heroin addiction has been stopped. For the slum-born, minority-group addict, Drs. Dole and Nyswander have pointed out, "a therapeutic team with a range of skills is needed to deal with his social and legal problems. Physicians, nurses, vocational counselors, older patients, and legal advisers bring essential skills to the task. This may not be true of the middle-class addict who presents psychiatric rather than social problems. Such a patient probably will respond better to an individual therapist rather than to a team."

An index of the care with which Drs. Dole and Nyswander deal with the rehabilitation process is the degree of detailed documentation of each patient throughout all phases of the methadone project. The drug status of every patient is determined objectively by daily urine tests for the first six weeks, and there are at least weekly urine tests thereafter. These tests detect heroin taking, amphetamines, some tranquilizers, and barbiturates. "In addition," they point out, "the data office tabulates reports obtained weekly from the clinical staff and supplementary data from staff, police, welfare, employers, and family. No other program has comparable data."

In New York City the methadone program has continued to expand. In the spring of 1967, there were three inpatient units—at Manhattan General, at Harlem Hospital, and at Van Etten Hospital in the Bronx (for addicts with tuberculosis). There is also a growing number of outpatient units, functioning in rented office space in a variety of neighborhoods. No more than seventy-five patients are included in each of the outpatient units, thereby making it possible for the staff to keep track of every patient.

By March, 1967, there were 350 addicts in the program, with long waiting lists. During the preceding three years, 383 heroin addicts had been admitted. For the 33 who had been dropped or had left on their own, the failure of the program was due to psychopathic behavior not related to heroin use, intractable continuing addiction to alcohol or barbiturates, or psychosis. Most of the 33 have reapplied for admittance. Drs. Dole and Nyswander suggest that, for the future, "a more comprehensive program, with special facilities for psychopaths and a separate unit for mixed addiction, might succeed in helping some of these more complicated patients."

Of those who stayed in the program, not one became readdicted to heroin. Included were fifty women, usually among the most difficult addicts to rehabilitate. Seventy-eight percent of the 350 were either employed or at school or both. The others were either too new on the program or unemployable. For the unemployables, Drs. Nyswander and Dole say, "the minimum goal is that they live decently, with support if necessary from public welfare or from relatives."

After examining these results, a medical committee evaluating the program for the City of New York recommended in March, 1967, that the methadone program be given additional funds to include one thousand addicts. (During the previous three years, because of the limitation of staff and resources, seven addicts died while awaiting admittance to the program. One of the seven was arrested on a Friday in the week before he was to start. The next day, in jail, he hung himself.)

Other cities and states are expressing interest in the program, and as Dr. Nyswander says, "the methadone blockage procedure for treatment of heroin addiction is emerging from the protective isolation of its research label. The original questions as to its safety and effectiveness have been answered. And the steadily increasing number of applications from addicts now on the street gives reason to hope that a significant proportion of the street addicts will welcome this opportunity to escape heroin addiction. It's a treatment that appeals especially to those now considered hard-core criminal addicts who have repeatedly relapsed after withdrawal."

There has been one other result of the methadone treatment program. In the course of it, Dr. Marie Nyswander and Dr. Vincent P. Dole were married.

AS MORE experience has been gained in the use of methadone to block heroin addiction, a basic objection to the procedure has been made on the grounds that methadone substitutes one addiction for another.

The Reverend Stephen Chinlund, Associate Director of the East Harlem Protestant Parish Narcotics Office, has asked whether the methadone treatment "may so tranquilize all the anxieties that any kind of realistic therapy is impossible and the addict finally confronting Dr. Nyswander is only half a man. He has neither the flamboyant qualities nor the brusque honesty which she finds so attractive . . . nor does the addict have a new start on life in the full possession of his faculties.

Can he form serious, loyal, human relationships while using methadone? Can he really marry and have a family? If he is a student or a musician, is his work better on methadone than it would be if he were fully rehabilitated and not requiring the use of massive doses of a narcotic drug? These are questions which at best remain unanswered, but there are psychiatrists and other medical men who say today that the properties of methadone are such that the only benefits of such a program come to the general public because men on methadone have been drugged into a semivegetable state."

Reverend Chinlund opts instead for a treatment of addiction which would, as he puts it, permit former addicts "to live as free men, making their own choices within the limits of the law; not dependent on syringes of heroin or methadone; not dependent on doctors or priests; but self-reliant human beings in the pattern of interdependencies which form a broad healthy society."

Dr. Nyswander answers by observing that this objection is a corollary of the statement that giving methadone to a heroin addict is like giving an alcoholic rum instead of scotch. "However," she says, "if you give rum rather than scotch to an alcoholic, does his health or behavior improve in any way? Of course, it does not. The facts are that methadone, as it is used in our project, makes those people taking it as 'normal' in their capacities—emotional and otherwise—as you or I. To talk of their being 'drugged into a semivegetable state' ignores our repeated experience that there is no way in which anyone can tell a patient on methadone from someone who is not on the drug—except by a urine test.

"This argument is also part of the tradition which claims that an addict cannot be rehabilitated or 'cured' until and unless he is drug-free. But you cannot medically rehabilitate a diabetic unless and until you control his diabetes through the use of insulin. In our area, moreover, we are dealing with a pharmacological addiction. And it's because so many addicts in the past have been unable to overcome this chemical addiction that psychotherapy and other forms of treatment have shown poor results. Now it may be, and this is part of the next stage of research, that the action of methadone may be able to reverse the syndrome of heroin-craving. In that case, patients might not have to remain on methadone. And that's another reason for my saying that the whole field of addiction has been opened for medical research because of methadone.

"But as for the present, the criterion for any effort at rehabilitation is how well—how normally—the patients function in a community. Again the facts are that patients on methadone are able to form and sustain 'serious, loyal, human relationships.' Social workers in the program have the satisfying task of helping families to reconcile. Children return to their families, and parents begin to accept their sons back into family activity. Patients come to the clinics with their wives or bring their children in with them. New cars appear, new clothes are proudly bought, old debts are repaid. Most of our patients, in fact, can be counted on to put in ten to twenty hours a week in overtime on their jobs. And, as I've said, these patients have not lost that extra dimension of perception from having been so far down—in society and into themselves. They retain their honesty and their humor.

"To talk of their being half human also ignores the pride that characterizes these patients. Pride in their jobs, in their renewed family ties, in their appearance. Some with tracks are asking for plastic surgery to remove those traces of the past. They are very much, very fully alive. At Christmastime, for example, we can especially see how much life has been regained for the patients and for their families. They all come in, with their families, to express thanks to the staff and we realize that while we've been helping one patient, there have been a wife, two children, two sets of parents, and numerous brothers and sisters, all of whom are now celebrating for the first time in many years.

"By all measurements, our patients are thoroughly functioning as members of their community. Their employment rate, for one example, is 50 percent higher than that of the economic groups from which they came. And out of fifty women in our program so far, not one has been arrested since they've been part of the program. And yet all had been prostitutes. Forty-two percent of the women are working, 40 percent are housewives, 12 percent are on public assistance, and 2 percent are students. 'Half a man' or 'half a woman' indeed! From all our tests and observations, there is no evidence, moreover, that methadone produces either any tranquilizing effect or any artificial drive. There are times when I might wish methadone did have a tranquilizing effect, as when one of our patients, accompanied by a counselor, is going out for a job for the first time and is perspiring as well as carrying a paper bag in case he vomits out of nervousness.

"I'm not saying that all the patients on methadone are without problems. Many still have the social problems which are connected with the neighborhoods in which they grew up and the poor schooling they received. But heroin craving is no longer a problem. There is also a small group of middle-class patients in serious need of psychiatric help, and they have become our most difficult cases. Methadone does not cure emotional problems. But now, for the first time, because of methadone, we can see who needs what kind of help. And on the basis of our experience so far, few of the so-called lower-class addicts need psychiatric attention. They need help getting schooling and jobs, and that's what we're trying to give them. We do need bigger programs to help these patients get better vocational skills. We need more industries to open their doors to them. We need more schools to set up the kinds of classes in which our patients can be comfortable.

"But the point is that because of methadone, our patients are now able to utilize this help so that they can indeed become 'self-reliant human beings in the pattern of interdependencies which form a broad healthy society.' "

I would add that my own observations of and conversations with a number of patients on methadone fail to support the assumption that they are in a "semivegetable" state. On the contrary, they are alert, fully responsive and, as Dr. Nyswander notes, proud. Proud of being reborn as one of them puts it. Proud of no longer being "some kind of animal," another says.

At one hospital I talked with a Puerto Rican in his late twenties. He had been an addict since his teens, had never worked, had been in and out of prisons, and for several years while on the street slept anywhere he could. Now on methadone, he has been a valued employee of the hospital as a ward clerk for nearly a year. He also speaks at medical societies about methadone and has helped open up a number of job opportunities for other patients by visiting and speaking at publishing houses, department stores, social agencies, universities, and factories.

I also spent some time with a number of women patients. From a life of addiction financed by prostitution, they had become reunited with their families, had found jobs, and in some cases, had gone back to school. One of them described another young woman's experience: "It used to be that when Angela came into her house, her mother would shake. She'd hide everything she could, first of all her pocketbook. Now it's all changed. She's working, she has no craving left for heroin, she's had her teeth fixed, she cares how she dresses, and she's really got a home again."

Another patient, a young man, had been told by his father three years before, "I don't want to see you anymore, I don't even want you at my funeral." For the past two years, the man has been on methadone, is working and supporting his family, and is now a business associate of his father. The father called Dr. Nyswander at one point and said, "For the first time in many years, I have a son once more."

For those who have stayed with the methadone program, rehabilitation has clearly taken place if the criterion for rehabilitation is the ability to function responsibly in the community and the ability to sustain family relationships. As for the moral question—are they not still addicted, though not to herion? I would suggest that critics such as Reverend Chinlund try to be somewhat more cautious in being judgmental. Role reversal might be indicated. If the Reverend can imagine himself in the place of the patient, he might then contrast his present sense of self with his self-appraisal during the years of addiction to heroin. To insist that no "real" rehabilitation has taken place until an addict is absolutely drug-free sets up an absolute standard of self-reliance that may have a great deal more relevance to the Reverend than to the patient. And it evades a more complicated moral problem. In many instances, patients on methadone have been helped by none of the other current alternatives—from Synanon to civil commitment. What is the Reverend to tell them? "Even though you are now functioning well, keep trying the more 'moral' alternatives?" For whose purpose? For the Reverend and his stake in moral absolutes? Or for the patient and his stake in making a life that is meaningful to him?

It may be that eventually the question will be academic. As Dr. Nyswander suggests, further research on methadone or on another drug may make it possible to remove all memory in the body of the craving for heroin and then a blockade treatment would no longer be necessary for the pharmacological aspect of the problem. It may also be that after additional years of experience with patients on methadone, some or many will decide to withdraw themselves from methadone. But in terms of the present and of coming back into society again, who is to say that those methadone patients now at work and at school and with their families are any less "moral" than other addicts who have found Synanon or some other drug-free treatment successful?

129

There will indeed be those who make that distinction. They will discount the contention that for some, addiction is a chronic pharmacological problem. They will point instead to those addicts who have withdrawn themselves from all drugs and have remained off drugs. It is a remarkable assumption—that all addicts *could* be "clean" if sufficiently and suitably "motivated"—in view of the evidence so far. But let us grant that assumption for argument's sake. Is, then, self-reliance absolutely synonymous with being drug-free? What, then, are the other absolute criteria of self-reliance? I have a question, for example, whether the need to believe in a God indicates absolute self-reliance.

But there are those in this world who keep the kind of moral ledger which makes it easy to answer the question: is not addiction in itself, whether to methadone or to heroin, the basic problem? And is not the basic goal the extirpation of addiction? I expect it would be less easy to ask that question the longer one spent time in the company of addicts on methadone. But in this, as in all other rehabilitative preserves, each cadre of solution-seekers usually stays within the confines of its own vested experience and criteria of "progress." It would be too dangerous to look outside for too long. In dealing with addicts, as Dr. Nyswander has said, "You have to be careful you're not writing a contract in which you give them something and you want something back."

WHEN the City of New York decided to expand the methadone program in March, 1967, Dr. Donald B. Louria, a member of the medical evaluation committee which made that decision, emphasized: "We couldn't go out into the street and pick up any 350 addicts and expect the same results. This is not a cure-all."

Dr. Nyswander agrees: "No one treatment in medicine is good for everyone. Synanon, for one example, has a great deal to offer some of those who have other problems besides addiction and lack of educational and vocational skills. Other centers, like Daytop Lodge, which also involve long periods of self-examination with the aid of other addicts in a kind of group therapy environment, can be of considerable use to some patients."

And the Reverend Chinlund, whose narcotics center is now operating Exodus House, a residence rehabilitation facility in East Harlem for the comprehensive treatment of drug-free addicts, makes the valid point that "we have no final answer. Neither does anyone else. There are some ways of working which will be more helpful to one addict than another. But let us not cut short our search for ways of treatment. We must continue to seek realistic solutions before we abdicate either to cries of despair or to an announcement of The Answer."

The "realism," however, of the present trend in New York and several other states toward compulsory civil commitment of addicts is extremely doubtful. First, the overwhelming weight of evidence is that an addict must want to be "cured" or rehabilitated before any approach can work. Secondly, most of the civil commitment plans require the hospitals and rehabilitation centers involved to be located outside the cities and thereby outside the home environments of the addicts. This provision, as New York State Senators Basil Paterson and Whitney Seymour have pointed out, "is an open invitation to failure. If an addict is to be prepared to adjust to society he must do so where he is accustomed to living, not in a foreign environment." And thirdly, as the New York Civil Liberties Union has emphasized, compulsory commitment violates basic constitutional rights of the addict. It permits arrest, for example, without evidence that the prisoner has committed a crime or is even an addict—a violation of the "search and seizure" provision of the Eighth Amendment. And by denying the alleged addict an opportunity to "seek treatment of his own choice and doctors of his own choice," it violates the "due process of law" section of the Fourteenth Amendment. Furthermore, compulsory medical examination and interrogation during an involuntary custodial confinement violates the "self-incrimination" provision of the Fifth Amendment. (For a comprehensive analysis of problems in constitutional law concerning all civil commitment procedures, not only New York State's, see "Civil Commitment of Narcotic Addicts," *The Yale Law Journal*, Volume 76, Number 6, May, 1967.)

On the other hand, there is a broadening spectrum of approaches to treatment which do not require the isolation of the addict and some of which do not insist that rehabilitation can begin only when the addict is drug-free. As Leon Brill, Project Director of the Washington Heights Rehabilitation Center in New York City, writes in the June, 1966, *International Journal of Addictions*: "We are currently veering between two points of reference: the old one of total abstinence, and the newer one of viewing narcotic addiction as within the purview of other emotional illnesses, with emphasis on the adjustment of addicts even regardless of the achievement of total abstinence in the community. We are, finally, feeling freer on a pilot basis to try all approaches, including ambulatory maintenance programs, which would serve to bring narcotic addiction in line with other mental illnesses, psychoses, depressions, currently being treated by psychoactive, ataractic, and anti-depressive drugs. We must shed the blinders of our long-standing stereotypes to permit ourselves the freedom to experiment, research, evaluate—do all the things necessary to accumulate the scientific knowledge we need to cope with the addiction problem."

For those who say "ambulatory maintenance programs" are impossible because addiction requires ever-increasing quantities of whatever drug is used, Dr. Vincent Dole answers that quite apart from methadone, "with a large number of untested 'narcotic' drugs now available and a continuing discovery of new varieties, the statement, frequently made, that maintenance treatment of addiction has been tried and proved a failure seems preposterous." For one example, there is the nonaddictive drug, cyclazocine, which substantially reduces the physiological impact of morphine-based narcotics by preventing the morphine from reaching the receptor sites in the nervous system. Initial research at this point is too thin to warrant any substantial judgments as to the effectiveness of cyclazocine as a way of blocking heroin, but its existence illustrates Dr. Dole's point that chemical discoveries in this area are just beginning.

For some addicts, psychiatry may well prove helpful. Such has been the experience of the Psychiatric Hospital in Rio Piedras, Puerto Rico, which utilizes psychological testing and intensive group therapy. Dr. Brill sees expanding opportunities for treatment of addicts, psychiatric as well as other forms of care, in the growing move toward community health centers which are coordinating a number of resources into one nucleus. And as part of treatment in a community center, I would add, physicians with training in addiction could be authorized to administer methadone or other drugs so that addicts not ready or able to get off drugs could concentrate on the insights they might get from therapy and other aids without having to be concerned with a craving for heroin.

Nor would it be necessary for all addicts to get their care at community health centers or clinics. Physicians trained in the methadone program, or in other forms of treatment involving drugs, could treat the addict as part of their regular private practice. For that to happen, as the American Civil Liberties Union has emphasized, there must be changes in Narcotics Bureau regulations to incorporate the U.S. Supreme Court's 1925 ruling in *Linder* v. *United States* which does allow a physician to treat an addict lawfully with drugs.

With regard to rehabilitation, whether the addict is off or on drugs, there is a considerable area for exploration in the use of community houses and halfway houses to provide a protected environment, within his own neighborhood, for a man on the way back into society. Dr. Nyswander, along with others, has also suggested more sheltered workshops where "carpenters, plumbers, and other specialists could teach techniques to the addict, take him under their wing, and guide him into the world of work. If we owned a factory in East Harlem, we could help as many addicts as applied. They could work as they learned a skill."

"The urgent need now," Nathan Straus III, president of the National Association for the Prevention of Addiction to Narcotics, underlines, "is for a broad program of research and experimentation to find answers to many questions basic to an understanding of the problem. If we are to achieve substantial progress, it is essential that scientists, physicians, psychologists, social scientists, and other qualified professionals participate on a wide scale in the field of drug addiction, and work directly with addicts living in their home environment. There is today a serious lack of qualified professional personnel, particularly doctors, required for any large, worthwhile program. Therefore intensive efforts must be made to induce young physicians and scientists to build careers in this new and exciting field. Particular emphasis should be placed on a large number of scientific experiments in the treatment of addicts on an outpatient basis, under the direction of qualified medical institutions."

Meanwhile the work of Drs. Nyswander and Dole continues. In New York, their methadone approach has been accredited by the New York State Narcotic Addict Commission, which now funds it as a treatment procedure. Accordingly, its name is now the Methadone Maintenance Treatment Program. (It began as the Methadone Maintenance Research Project.) As of October, 1967, the program has had experience with five hundred patients, and fifty more are being added every six weeks. Much more funds will be required for expansion and for training of additional staff as there is still a two year waiting list for admission.

In the spring of 1967, Drs. Nyswander and Dole were

135

invited to England, Denmark, and Sweden to advise in the setting up of the methadone programs which are now under way in those countries. Another program will soon be instituted in Burma. Both doctors remain eager in their intent to go beyond treatment and rehabilitation of addicts to find out the very nature of addiction. "Now that we have methadone to work with," Dr. Nyswander says, "it's sort of like when the microscope was discovered. That was the tool which enabled scientists to begin finding out about the causes of infectious diseases. You could *see* bacteria. Now we're going to be able to *see* what addiction is and how it works."

ABOUT THE AUTHOR:

NAT HENTOFF is a staff writer for *The New Yorker*, where a shorter version of A Doctor Among the Addicts aroused intense interest among both medical and lay readers. Mr. Hentoff is the author of six previous books, the most recent of which was *Our Children Are Dying*, an account of a New York City school principal. Born in Boston, Massachusetts, Mr. Hentoff attended Northeastern University and Harvard Graduate School with further work at the Sorbonne.